INDIE *ROCK*

FINDING AN INDEPENDENT VOICE

THE MUSIC LIBRARY

By Vanessa Oswald

Portions of this book originally appeared in
The History of Indie Rock by Jennifer Skancke.

LUCENT PRESS

Published in 2019 by
Lucent Press, an Imprint of Greenhaven Publishing, LLC
353 3rd Avenue
Suite 255
New York, NY 10010

Copyright © 2019 Greenhaven Press, a part of Gale, Cengage Learning
Gale and Greenhaven Press are registered trademarks used herein under license.

All new materials copyright © 2019 Lucent Press, an Imprint of Greenhaven Publishing, LLC.

All rights reserved. No part of this book may be reproduced in any form without permission in writing from the publisher, except by a reviewer.

Designer: Deanna Paternostro
Editor: Vanessa Oswald

Cataloging-in-Publication Data

Names: Oswald, Vanessa.
Title: Indie rock: finding an independent voice / Vanessa Oswald.
Description: New York : Lucent Press, 2019. | Series: The music library | Includes index.
Identifiers: ISBN 9781534565203 (pbk.) | ISBN 9781534565210 (library bound) | ISBN 9781534565227 (ebook)
Subjects: LCSH: Alternative rock music–History and criticism–Juvenile literature.
Classification: LCC ML3534.O79 2019 | DDC 781.66–dc23

Printed in the United States of America

CPSIA compliance information: Batch #BW19KL: For further information contact Greenhaven Publishing LLC, New York, New York at 1-844-317-7404.

Please visit our website, www.greenhavenpublishing.com. For a free color catalog of all our high-quality books, call toll free 1-844-317-7404 or fax 1-844-317-7405.

Table of
Contents

Foreword	4
Introduction *Indie Rock Phenomenon*	6
Chapter One *Punk Rock Attitude*	12
Chapter Two *The Power of DIY*	26
Chapter Three *Explosion of College Rock*	38
Chapter Four *The Emergence of Grunge Music*	50
Chapter Five *Indie Rock Is Born*	63
Chapter Six *Indie Rock Innovations*	76
Notes	92
Essential Albums	96
For More Information	98
Index	100
Picture Credits	103
About the Author	104

Foreword

Music has a unique ability to speak to people on a deeply personal level and to bring people together. Whether it is experienced through playing a favorite song on a smartphone or at a live concert surrounded by thousands of screaming fans, music creates a powerful connection that sends songs to the top of the charts and artists to the heights of fame.

Music history traces the evolution of those songs and artists. Each generation of musicians builds on the one that came before, and a strong understanding of the artists of the past can help inspire the musical superstars of the future to continue to push boundaries and break new ground.

A closer look at the history of a musical genre also reveals its impact on culture and world events. Music has inspired social change and ignited cultural revolutions. It does more than simply reflect the world; it helps to shape the world.

Music is often considered a universal language. A great song or album speaks to people regardless of age, race, economic status, or nationality. Music from various artists, genres, countries, and time periods might seem completely different at first, but certain themes can be found in all kinds of music: love and loss, success and failure, and life and death. In discovering these similarities, music fans are able to see how many things we all have in common.

Each style of music has its own story, and those stories are filled with colorful characters, shocking events, and songs with true staying power. The Music Library presents those stories to readers with the help of those who know the stories best—music critics, historians, and artists. Annotated quotes by these experts give readers an inside look at a wide variety of musical styles—from early hip-hop and classic country to today's chart-topping pop hits and indie rock favorites. Readers with a passion for music—whether they are headbangers or lovers of

Latin music—will discover fun facts about their favorite artists and gain a deeper appreciation for how those artists were influenced by the ones who paved the way in the past.

The Music Library is also designed to serve as an accessible introduction to unfamiliar genres. Suggestions for additional books and websites to explore for more information inspire readers to dive even further into the topics, and the essential albums in each genre are compiled for superfans and new listeners to enjoy. Photographs of some of music's biggest names of the past and present fill the pages, placing readers in the middle of music history.

All music tells a story. Those stories connect people from different places, cultures, and time periods. In understanding the history of the stories told through music, readers discover an exciting way of looking at the past and develop a deeper appreciation for different voices.

INTRODUCTION

Indie Rock
Phenomenon

Indie rock is a genre of alternative rock music that developed in opposition to mainstream rock music and culture. Designated indie (or independent) scenes sprouted up in several cities in the United States and United Kingdom (UK), and from there, more indie scenes developed outside of these countries.

Death Cab for Cutie started out as an obscure indie rock band from Bellingham, Washington. By 2006, however, many fans of popular music were likely to say that Death Cab for Cutie was one of the most popular bands in the indie rock scene. The band showed up on numerous top-10 lists of indie rock groups. Their music was played frequently on commercial radio stations and was even featured on popular television shows such as *The O.C.* and *Six Feet Under* and in the 2005 movie *Wedding Crashers*. In just a few years, Death Cab for Cutie rose from relative obscurity to become one of the most recognizable bands in America.

Death Cab for Cutie formed in 1997 and released their first four albums on Seattle's independent record label, Barsuk Records. Known for their dreamy pop sound, created by a combination of electronic music with vocals and guitars, the band appealed to a large underground audience as well as to critics of independent music.

The band's fourth album, *Transatlanticism*, which was released in 2003, sold 225,000 copies in the first year. Suddenly, the relatively unknown band was receiving attention from the media and major record labels, which wanted to capitalize on the band's underground popularity. One year later, the band signed with Atlantic Records, a major label in the music industry, and they officially broke into the mainstream music world. In 2005, their song "Soul Meets Body" from their *Plans* album reached number 60 on the Billboard Hot 100, while the album reached number 4 on Billboard's Top Albums Chart. Death Cab for Cutie

Death Cab for Cutie is one of the most well-known indie rock bands. They started out releasing music solely on independent record labels and were later recognized and promoted by major labels.

represents just one of many indie rock bands that exemplify the growing popularity of the independent music scene.

Critics and music fans vary in their opinions about whether bands such as Death Cab for Cutie are still technically indie rock since they are no longer signed to an independent label. Originally, being on an independent label had been the defining characteristic of the indie rock genre. Indie rock was a term new to most Americans in the late 1990s. The term described bands and artists who were making rock music on independent labels outside of the mainstream. Now that indie rock has entered into the mainstream, many critics wonder what will happen to the independent scene that gained its identity as the alternative to the pop and rock music industries.

No One Specific Sound

Indie rock is difficult to define not only because of crossover appeal but also because the music has never had a specific sound, unlike other musical genres such as jazz, blues, or country. There are no telltale sounds such as country music's guitar twang or signature motifs such as jazz's improvisations. Although indie rock is a form of rock and roll and uses guitars, basses, and drums in the basic band unit, the music encompasses a wide range of sounds. For instance, the White Stripes were a minimalist rock duo from Detroit, Michigan, playing simple compositions with a guitar, piano, and drums. The Decemberists from Portland, Oregon, however, are a five-piece band that uses instruments such as the accordion and upright bass. Though quite different in their sounds and approaches, both bands are considered part of the indie rock genre's history.

What makes the White Stripes and the Decemberists indie rock, then? Most frequently, indie rock refers to rock music made by bands who are signed to an independent record label. Indie labels are considered to be any label other than one of the "Big Three" record

The Decemberists are an indie rock band comprised of five members that formed in 2000 in Portland, Oregon.

companies, which are Universal Music Group, Sony Music Entertainment, and Warner Music Group, or their affiliates, which are smaller labels owned by the Big Three. EMI Group used to be listed as a major record label, with the groups being referred to as the "Big Four." However, in December 2011, EMI Group was absorbed by Sony Music Entertainment and Universal Music Group, which left the "Big Three." According to a 2016 report, these three labels hold about 62.4 percent of the U.S. music market, which means 62.4 percent of all music sold, streamed, or downloaded worldwide is distributed by one of these three labels. These labels also own their own distribution channels, giving them a lot of control over the recording and marketing of music.

Independent labels have provided an alternative for those artists who find it difficult to get a recording contract with one of the major labels. These independent labels are smaller than the major labels and typically take chances on new groups as well as bands who make music that does not fit the pop market. There is a lot more room for experimentation on indie labels, whereas artists signed to one of the major labels are often tightly controlled by the company. As such, indie artists are able to maintain some degree of creative control over the sound and distribution of their music.

The Purist Model

The expansion of indie record labels—and ultimately indie rock—in the 1990s had a lot to do with the dissatisfaction many musicians and artists felt with the major record labels. Some artists were concerned that the labels had all the power when it came to making and selling music. Others were put off by the fact that major labels often were not interested in music that they did not think would immediately capture the attention of the buying public. Many artists and bands preferred to make music that was different from music receiving mass airplay and often experimented with new sounds and instrumentation. These artists were soon called independent.

As such, indie rock has often been thought of by those in the independent music scene as being "purer" and "less corporatized" than mainstream pop music. Perhaps due to the rise of the independent label scene in the late 1970s and early 1980s as an alternative to the corporate rock scene—in which bands were often created by the studios or else had their sounds altered and streamlined to achieve marketability—indie rock has been acclaimed as being more creative and artistic because it is supposedly less manufactured than some of the music put out by major labels. Indie rock has gained a reputation for being the ideal way of making music because indie rock artists tend to experiment, write their own music and lyrics, and avoid overproduction. Scholar Ryan Hibbett described indie rock's appeal as outsider music:

> *Because indie rock gains its appeal through its defiance of mainstream conventions, because it does not meet the protocols for radio or music television ... it cannot achieve a mass following. Thus indie enthusiasts turn to symbolic value, defending what they like as "too good" for radio, too innovative and challenging to interest those blasting down the highway. They become the scholars and conservators of "good" music.*[1]

Indie rock fans tend to believe that their favorite musicians are less concerned with being rock stars and are more interested in making music without compromise. Many artists, in fact, claim that they choose to remain independent rather than become part of the mainstream so that their artistic vision will not be warped by corporate pressures. As a result, this ideal of purity is attributed to indie rock.

Although plenty of bands stick to this independent ethic, many indie rock artists use independent labels as stepping-stones to signing with major labels. Sometimes bands start out on an indie label and then build a large enough fan base to attract a major label. Once the group's music is available to the public, most bands ultimately seek the recognition and money offered by a major label deal. Some indie music purists consider those indie rock musicians who have signed with a major label sellouts—meaning they have forgone their independent ideals to achieve fame and make a lot of money.

The purist ideal further complicates indie rock and blurs the boundary between maintaining artistic idealism and taking advantage of an opportunity for mainstream success. This issue raises several difficult questions: Is a band that starts out on an independent label still technically indie if they sign with a major label? What if the band keeps their independent ethic and sense of experimentation; would or should they still be considered an indie rock band?

Cycles of Rock

While some argue about whether being signed to an independent label or having an independent spirit qualifies a band as indie rock, others see indie rock as nothing but a marketing ploy to sell music. Music, particularly rock music, tends to evolve in cycles. Eventually, what is popular in the mainstream becomes tired and old, and record companies look to tap into the newest underground rock music being played by teenagers in small local scenes. Once the industry latches on to successful underground music, they need a term to categorize it so that it has a place in music stores and on commercial radio.

Indie rock is the latest music in this cycle of renewal. In the 1960s, psychedelic music brought a counterculture to mainstream awareness, as did punk in the 1970s, hardcore and college rock in the 1980s, and grunge in the early 1990s. Indie rock evolved to become what it is as a result of significant developments in the music industry during these earlier periods of music. For instance, indie rock is youth-driven music much like punk was in the middle-to-late 1970s. It draws on the do-it-yourself ethic defined by the British underground punk scene and the American hardcore scene in the late 1970s and early 1980s. Like college rock did in the 1980s, indie rock taps into the youth market through college radio stations and networks of educated youth. Similar to the grunge movement in the early 1990s, indie rock faces commercialization now that the term has been co-opted by the recording industry to sell music.

The historical connections illustrate that indie rock has strong roots, but as with grunge, the flowering of indie rock might signal its eventual demise. More optimistic observers contend, however, that it is just one more cycle in the ever-changing rock music scene. When the current indie rock music is picked up by the mainstream, like psychedelic music was in the 1960s and grunge was in the 1990s, it will drive other musicians underground, and a new music scene will emerge. For now, indie rock is alive and well, yet in the future, the search to discover a new rock genre awaits.

CHAPTER ONE

Punk Rock
Attitude

A new genre of music—known as punk rock music—emerged in the mid-1970s and was one of the first to influence the creation of indie rock. This type of music shocked the masses with its brash and sometimes vulgar attitude and aesthetic. Punk rock was heavily rooted in 1960s garage rock and proto-punk, both music movements that demonstrated a do-it-yourself work ethic and style. Punk rock was the alternative to mainstream rock music of the time.

In November 1976, the Sex Pistols, an unheard-of punk rock band from London, England, released their first record single, "Anarchy in the U.K." The song, which reached number 38 on the UK singles chart, was an angry rant at the failures of the British government. It encouraged people to defy the government and live in a state of absolute freedom. Lead singer Johnny Rotten screamed the lyrics while proclaiming to be the Antichrist. Many people in England were terrified by the band's message. Their public behavior, including swearing on live television, and the near riots that followed their performances also contributed to the band's bad reputation. Never before had a band expressed their anger so blatantly. The media immediately took notice, and the Sex Pistols were featured on the front pages of newspapers and magazines with headlines such as "The Filth and the Fury." Almost overnight, punk rock music, which had until then existed in small underground music circles, entered the consciousness of mainstream audiences.

Though there were punk bands before the Sex Pistols, they popularized punk rock music and helped turn it into a popular music genre. Countless punk rock bands were formed in the wake of the Sex Pistols' popularity. Punk rock became an anthem for the disillusioned young people who identified with the anger and energy of the music. It allowed young people an outlet to express their dissatisfaction with society and the expectations placed on them. Punk rock also encouraged individuality, a quality that many young people felt had been lacking in mainstream rock and roll. Lyrics questioned the state of society and told listeners that things did not have to be as they seemed. Music critic Greil Marcus defined punk as treason "against the future society had planned for you; against your own impulse to say yes, to buy whatever others had put on the market ... Punk was a new music, a new social critique, but most of all it was a new kind of free speech."[2]

Although the first wave of punk rock lasted only a few short years, it laid the foundation for the indie rock scene that would emerge years later. Like indie rock, punk was initially outsider music that spoke to the youth. It was music that young people identified with and could call their own. Punk made being independent and speaking for oneself essential qualities in all youth music scenes that followed. In fact, this ideal would become the cornerstone of the development of the independent music scene.

Mainstream Rock and Roll

The term "punk rock" was developed around 1976 to describe the loud, fast, and angry music that was emerging as an alternative to mainstream rock-and-roll music. By the early 1970s, rock and roll had existed for close to two decades and had developed into a major commodity. Popular rock bands such as the Who, the Rolling Stones, and the Beatles were heavily promoted by their record labels. These bands dominated radio airwaves and embarked on major tours, selling out stadium-size venues to adoring fans. Record labels scrambled to sign similar acts in the hope of making a lot of money.

The popular rock bands at the time were tightly controlled by their record companies. The music was produced in elaborate recording studios using the latest studio technology to enhance the sound of a band's vocals and their instruments. Like all industries, the music industry tried to copy successful formulas. Record executives were mainly interested in bands who would appeal to mainstream audiences, so many major-label groups had songs with similar-sounding guitar riffs and familiar chord patterns. In addition, most songs had to be at least 3 minutes long to be played on commercial radio. There was little room for bands who were interested in experimentation.

While the record labels catered to—and helped shape—popular tastes, many young listeners grew tired of hearing the same select, radio-friendly songs over and over. Young musicians were also disenchanted with an industry-controlled music scene in which success was measured by expensive studio production and arena touring. They began to explore alternatives to satisfy their musical cravings. Some bands retreated to the underground—a term referring to a loose affiliation of artists who could not or did not want to break into the mainstream. In the underground, people could play any kind of music they wanted and however they wanted to play it, which allowed for experimentation.

Underground Sounds

As more musicians gravitated toward playing this alternative style of rock and roll, many small underground scenes formed throughout England and America. Small clubs and venues that catered to more experimental music sprang up in cities such as London; New York City; Los Angeles, California; and San Francisco, California. One underground music scene that would be influential to the growing punk rock movement was the East Coast art and music scene that originated in New York in the mid-1960s.

The Velvet Underground was one of the most well-known and influential of the East Coast underground bands. The band was managed by pop culture artist Andy Warhol and would become known for their experimental sound and avant-garde influences. The band featured an electric viola, which was used to hold the same note, tone, or sound for lengthy periods of time and with little variation. Lead singer Lou Reed's lyrics were dark, confrontational, and grim, and they included suggestive and shocking subject matter that was not typically found in mainstream rock. He wrote graphic lyrics at a time when drug abuse and sexual identity were taboo subjects in popular culture. His songs contained darker images as opposed to the clean love ballads from teen pop idols.

The music and lyrics of the Velvet Underground did not capture the attention of record labels or commercial radio. The band was able to gain a small and dedicated cult following as a result of some of their shows, which were accompanied by Warhol's Pop Art imagery and included his unusual set of friends. Hibbett referred to these performances as "lo-fi yet highly experimental," making the Velvet Underground "an edgier and

The Velvet Underground was a rock band formed in the 1960s in New York City.

poorly received alternative to the Beatles."[3] The audiences for these events were typically comprised of like-minded youth who were excited by the cultish atmosphere and the newness of the sounds.

Many listeners were inspired to start their own bands after hearing the Velvet Underground. Iggy Pop, lead singer of the Stooges, was moved to make music after hearing the band's record *The Velvet Underground & Nico*. Pop remembers becoming aware that it was possible to create music despite not having any prior musical knowledge or training. He recalled, "That record became very key for me, not just for what it said, and for how great it was, but also because I heard other people who could make good music—without being any good at music. It gave me hope."[4]

PUNK ROCK ATTITUDE 15

Integration of Punk

Inspired by this underground music, many young people formed their own bands and began playing small clubs, especially in New York City. Clubs such as CBGB and Max's Kansas City allowed unsigned bands to play original music. It was in these small clubs in the early- to mid-1970s that youth-oriented audiences discovered a new sound that was speaking to them. As the scene gained momentum, this new style of music came to be known as punk rock.

Many of the early clubs featured the first punk acts, including Television, the New York Dolls, Patti Smith, Talking Heads, and the Ramones. These bands were not concerned with conformity and making music like popular rock bands. They were formed mainly of young people who had all been influenced by the counterculture of the 1960s and by the New York City art scene. These bands also distrusted authority and embraced the rebel outsider image to establish their identities and rejected popular music such as disco and the progressive rock groups who prized instrumentation and clean vocals. Many could not identify with what they saw as overproduced studio sounds. They wanted their rock and roll to be raw, similar to the garage bands who influenced them from the middle-to-late 1960s.

Several of the musicians who played these clubs had no previous musical training. Their shows depended on energy, visual interest, volume, and audience participation in intimate spaces. They often played hard, fast, and out of tune. For instance, the New York Dolls were considered by most to be inept musicians. They used heavy drumming, minimal rhythm guitar, and a lead guitarist who played unpredictable melodies. Lead singer David Johansen recalled, "People who saw the Dolls said … 'anybody can do this.' I think what the Dolls did as far as being an influence on punk was that we showed that anybody could do it."[5]

The Ramones were also a punk band who did not have a background in music. However, their use of distorted guitars and fast tempos to create a simplistic but aggressive sound would come to characterize the abrasive side of punk music. The band emphasized the rhythm guitar and highlighted short guitar solos. Repeated bass lines and loud, thundering drums contributed to the aggressive feel of the songs. They used offbeat humor in their lyrics and in song titles such as "Suzy Is a Headbanger" and "Pinhead." Like most punk bands at the time, the Ramones were overlooked by the mainstream music industry, but the band built up a dedicated underground following.

The Ramones began their rise to punk rock fame in 1974 in a part of Queens, New York, known as Forest Hills.

PUNK ROCK ATTITUDE

CBGB

In December 1973, Hilly Kristal opened a bar called CBGB and OMFUG, an abbreviation which stood for "Country, Bluegrass, Blues and Other Music for Uplifting Gormandizers." Initially, these music genres were what Kristal intended to feature in the bar, but the music he ended up showcasing gave birth to the punk and new wave movement in New York City. Later, the venue just became known as CBGB. Some of the venue's most famed acts include Blondie, the Ramones, the Misfits, Television, Patti Smith Group, the Cramps, the B-52s, Joan Jett & the Blackhearts, and Talking Heads. Sonic Youth's Thurston Moore recalled his first experience at CBGB:

> What struck me the most was the sheer bloody-mindedness of the artists, poets, filmmakers and musicians who were rubbing up against one another there. Whatever glamour there was on that stage, many of the artists were basically subsisting at poverty level. Fame had little to do with money, which the club infamously paid little of. But being there felt like you were at ground zero of the most critical listening room of the future.[1]

1. Thurston Moore, "Thurston Moore: The First Time I Saw Bands at CBGB (in 1976)," *New York Times*, May 2, 2017. www.nytimes.com/2017/05/02/arts/music/thurston-moore-sonic-youth-cbgb.html.

Safety-Pin Fashion

Not only did punk come to have a distinct sound, but it also became associated with a particular look. Many of these early punk bands created an image that appealed to young audiences. The look helped create an identity for those punk musicians as well as fans. Band members often used their clothing to distinguish themselves from the way mainstream artists dressed. The New York Dolls wore make-up and dressed like women, while the Ramones wore tight jeans, Converse Chuck Taylor high-top shoes, and black leather jackets. However, Richard Hell, a member of the Neon Boys, Television, and the Heartbreakers before forming Richard Hell and the Voidoids, would have the strongest impact on the punk look.

Hell created what some critics came to call the safety-pin ethic. Hell styled his hair into tall spikes and wore torn clothes that he fastened together with safety pins. Hell believed that fashion should be cheap and accessible rather than flashy and expensive, such as the outfits worn by most disco

CBGB was a legendary punk music club, which hosted several music acts who later became famous. The venue closed its doors in 2006.

fans and rock musicians. The tattered-and-torn look would become a punk staple later in the decade, especially after British entrepreneur Malcolm McLaren adopted the style and sold it in his London clothing shop. Some kids took the safety-pin ethic a step further and pierced their lips and ears with safety pins. Hell later described his interest in punk rock music and style:

> One thing I wanted to bring back to rock 'n' roll was the knowledge that you invent yourself… That's why I changed my name, why I did all the clothing style things, haircut, everything … That is the ultimate message of the New Wave [a term that is often used interchangeably with punk rock]: if you amass the courage that is necessary, you can completely invent yourself.[6]

British Punk Rock

The first New York punk rockers, such as the Ramones, the New York Dolls, and Television, were

The New York Dolls—formed in 1971—were one of the first bands in the New York City punk rock music scene.

the bands responsible for creating the punk sound and look, but it was Britain's punks who would bring punk music to the attention of mainstream America. New York punk gained a small and loyal following in the United States, but it did not get much

INDIE ROCK: FINDING AN INDEPENDENT VOICE

attention from the American public or the mainstream media. Despite the lack of media attention, many bands continued to make records, and some even embarked on small tours. Some of these tours visited England in the mid-1970s.

Britain's youth connected with the New York punk bands, especially the Ramones. The band's self-titled debut was one of the only punk records available to London's early punks. Many early British punk musicians learned to play instruments by playing along with the record. The arrangements were easy to learn in comparison to the relatively challenging chord structure found in popular rock music.

The aggressive sound of bands such as the Ramones also appealed to British youth. They adopted the punk sound and used it as a response to the hopelessness and anger they felt about the sociopolitical environment in Britain during the 1970s. Many of these punks were coming of age during great industrial unrest. A miner's strike from 1973 to 1974 and an Arab oil embargo around the same time limited production in England's factories. A lagging economy and high inflation rates made it difficult for many young people to find jobs. A conservative government was in place at the time, and many youth felt they had no chance to influence political change. This fueled a belief among young people that they lacked a future, and the despair resulted in a pessimistic and harsh outlook on life. Punk rock music became one outlet for expressing their discontent with society. This sense of doom is captured in the Sex Pistols' song "God Save the Queen" and the Clash's "London's Burning."

Punk was also a response to the boredom that many young people felt in their lives and how radio-friendly rock and roll had lost touch with those who no longer believed the 1960s ideals of love and drugs as the solutions to the world's problems. Steve Diggle of the Buzzcocks, a British punk group, described why punk proved to be the remedy to the boredom he felt:

The thing was, the musical landscape was dead. There was really nothing happening, and nothing relevant to the modern world. I mean it was 1976 when we started, and the progressive rock bands like Yes and Emerson, Lake, and Palmer were all sounding tired, and seemed to have run their course. They were singing about mushrooms in the sky and whatnot, and we were coming up to a million unemployed in this country [Britain]—which was a first—

and there was no excitement anywhere. We were 20 then, and we needed to question our lives, and make music that was relevant to our lives.[7]

The Sex Pistols

Many of Britain's youth turned to punk rock to create music that was relevant to them, including one of Britain's most notorious punk bands, the Sex Pistols. This band would solidify the rebellious attitude that became associated with punk rock. The band formed in 1975, and it was not long after that they developed a strong cult following due to their outrageous behavior. For example, a live television appearance in 1976 brought the band their first national exposure. Upset with one of the comments made by the host of the *Today* program, lead singer Johnny Rotten and guitarist Steve Jones swore on camera during the live taping. The tabloid press went wild, and the band topped the headlines. The incident caused many problems for the Sex Pistols during their tour to promote their single "Anarchy in the U.K." Local authorities canceled many of the Sex Pistols' concerts, and the press gave negative reviews for the rest. Some of the shows ended in riots. In another incident, the band played "God Save the Queen" (a song about the queen of England) from London's Thames River while following the queen's motorcade during the Royal Silver Jubilee celebration in 1977. They were arrested shortly after.

The Sex Pistols had a handful of singles and only one album in their two-year career. However, the band's ill-mannered behavior helped its music reach a generation of young people who identified with their rebellious attitude. The young punks' rejection of what they saw as bland, conformist society under the grips of an uncaring government held the youth together as much as the music. Joe Strummer of the Clash explained, "We're not going to go quietly to our deaths into some retirement home, eating Prozac. This is what they're [the leaders of society] planning for us, unless we do something about it. To always be a punk rocker is something everyone can do. And I mean that by attitude."[8]

Punk music encouraged its listeners to be strong-minded and independent. This mentality provided the backbone of punk music, which helped shape the early independent music movement. Diggle talked about how punk taught him to be independent:

It's given me strength not to

The Sex Pistols had a short-lived career—but a highly influential one.

be frightened of things in the world, you know? Punk gave me the strength to think, "Yeah, you can stand up and be counted, and do what you want in life, and not be hoodwinked by it all," in a simple, very general sweeping way. It gives you a sense to question things, and be positive, and open up. And that's what it's done for me, to realize you don't have to worry about people in power in society—in terms of how they can pressurize you and steer you in ways. It's made me fearless.[9]

Freedom of Punk

By the end of the 1970s, the punk movement was firmly established both in England and the United States. Punk offered an alternative to those youth who were bored with the current commercial culture or those who did not fit in or did not want to fit in with popular society. Punk also provided a

SID AND NANCY

Sid Vicious, bassist for the Sex Pistols, and Nancy Spungen were one of the punk scene's most notorious couples. After they met in London in 1977, the pair became inseparable. Spungen, who caused a lot of mayhem around the band, was banned from their 1978 tour. The former tour manager for the Heartbreakers said, "[S]he was a junkie, a drug supplier and an all-around lowlife … She was a very … bad influence on people who were already a mess. She was a troublemaker and a stirrer-upper."[1]

The Sex Pistols disbanded after the final show of their U.S. tour in January 1978, and Vicious and Spungen moved into New York City's Chelsea Hotel the following August. The Chelsea Hotel had been home to people such as Jackson Pollock, Bob Dylan, Patti Smith, and several other creative artists of the time.

On the night of October 11, 1978, Spungen was stabbed and died on the bathroom floor. Spungen's murder was never solved; however, there are several claims made about who might have killed her. Vicious, who had taken several drugs, was in a deep state of unconsciousness into the early morning hours. Initially, he was arrested and charged for the murder and confessed; however, he later denied it, claiming he was asleep when she died. In the months leading up to Vicious's trial for the murder, he died of a heroin overdose on February 2, 1979.

Rockets Redglare, who served as Vicious's bodyguard occasionally and also sold drugs, had delivered Dilaudids, an opioid painkiller, to Spungen the night of her death after she had asked for them. At 7:30 a.m., noises were heard from Spungen's room. At 10 a.m., Vicious had called down to the front desk of the hotel asking for help.

Some theories point to Redglare as the murderer. In his book, *Pretty Vacant: A History of Punk*, Phil Strongman claims Redglare tried to steal cash from the couple's hotel room and as Spungen tried to confront him, he stabbed her and left with the cash. Strongman also claims Redglare was later heard confessing about the theft and murder at CBGB.

1. Quoted in Jessica Wakeman, "Flashback: Nancy Spungen Found Dead at Chelsea Hotel," *Rolling Stone*, October 12, 2017. www.rollingstone.com/culture/news/flashback-nancy-spungen-found-dead-at-chelsea-hotel-w508409.

means of personal empowerment and introduced young people to the idea of making music on their own terms. Whether it was through the raucous sounds, the wild stage antics, or the political messages, the bands of the underground and punk rock era contributed to the ideology and spirit of future alternative rock movements, including indie rock.

These underground punk rockers inspired young musicians to follow in their footsteps and break away from social conventions and what was expected of them. These bands encouraged young people to be authentic individuals, experiment with music, and not be affected by what was popular in the mainstream music industry scene. As a result, the younger generation began starting bands on their own, and their new way of distribution was through independent record labels. This freedom from a major record label ignited creativity in these young artists and made them realize they could do it all on their own.

CHAPTER TWO

The Power of DIY

With underground music came the do-it-yourself (DIY) ethic. This was the mentality bands adopted when they realized they could produce albums on their own without the help and money of a major label. Also, the DIY aesthetic put more of a personalized stamp on the music and its packaging and publicity, which felt more exclusive for fans.

In the spring of 1979, an unknown London punk rock band by the name of the Homosexuals released their first self-recorded double single on their own Black Noise record label. Despite being unheard-of by the mainstream music press, the band sold 1,500 of the 2,000 copies they made of the single in 2 days. They did not advertise, they did not supply press handouts, and they did not send review copies to record labels and fan magazines, or fanzines. The band's music was not even played on the radio. However, the band was able—without the help of the mainstream music industry—to produce a relatively successful single.

The Homosexuals were part of the growing independent punk rock movement during the middle-to-late 1970s that promoted the DIY ethic. Bands such as the Sex Pistols and the Clash popularized punk rock with their antiestablishment and rebellious attitudes and showed people that anyone could be in a band, regardless of musical training. Bands such as the Homosexuals, however, took the independent spirit of punk rock further by producing their own records. These bands could play the music they wanted, and they did not have to rely on a record label to distribute or sell their music. By taking control of the recording process, these innovators showed that anybody who wanted to record an album could.

Recording independently was not entirely new. Garage bands had been making independent recordings since the 1960s, and independent record labels had existed since the beginning of the rock-and-roll movement. However, the independent label scene experienced a lull as the major labels swallowed them up in the late 1960s and early 1970s. As Britain's youth became disenchanted with the corporate hold on the recording industry, they looked back to the days of independent labels as an alternative to signing with a major label. Suddenly, kids all over Britain began making their own records.

Once the British punks demystified the recording process, American youth began forming their own small scenes built on the same grassroots DIY principles. In fact, DIY would become the foundation for the indie rock movement that would take place a couple of decades later. Some indie rock musicians today still adhere to the DIY ethic established by their predecessors.

Independent Record Labels

When the recording industry began to grow with the increasing popularity of rock and roll in the 1950s, it became diversified. There were plenty of record labels for artists to choose from, and the labels were owned by many different people with different tastes. This meant a variety of choices were available to musicians, and they could choose a label that best suited their personal and artistic interests. The distribution industry (through which records were made available to the people) was mostly independent too, so record companies could easily find eager distributors waiting to ship new products to the stores.

Through the 1950s and 1960s, then, it was relatively easy for an untested band to be signed by one of the many small, independent record labels. By the 1970s, however, the biggest record labels desired more control over the industry and began to look for ways to eliminate the competition. By the end of the decade, the major labels made distribution deals with some of the independent labels. In other cases, they started buying the independent labels outright. They also pumped a lot of money into promotion and advertising to overpower the independent competition and drove them out of business. They were largely able to do so because they had the financial power.

In the 1970s and 1980s, the music business was saturated with music from just five or six major labels. Many of these labels signed similar-sounding bands to compete with each other. It became difficult for bands to get a recording contract if they did not fit the mold. However, it was precisely the lack of opportunities for those interested in alternative styles of music that led to the rebirth of the independent record label movement in the late 1970s and early 1980s. Some of these labels were started by record store owners, music fans, and even musicians and artists. The artists and bands who created or produced music on these labels were considered to be part of an independent or alternative music scene. They either rejected the mainstream record business or were rejected by it and wanted to provide ways for musicians and artists to be heard.

First Indie Punk Bands

By the late 1970s, many of Britain's punks were fed up with the limited opportunities within the record industry. Many bands and artists felt rejected by the mainstream record industry, and they decided to take control of their own record distribution. The Buzzcocks and the Desperate Bicycles were the first two punk bands to make a record without the help of a major recording label. The Buzzcocks, a relatively inexperienced band, formed in Bolton, England, in 1976 after seeing the Sex Pistols in concert earlier that year. Within a matter of months, the band produced and released a four-track extended play (EP) album titled *Spiral Scratch* on its New Hormones label, which was founded by Buzzcocks manager Richard Boon and was the first independent punk rock label in the UK. The band recorded their songs at the local Indigo Sound Studios and pressed the result onto vinyl. By February 1977, they had released the album, which was not only the third UK punk record to be issued but also the first independent punk record ever recorded.

The Buzzcocks were one of the first punk bands. They formed in Bolton, England, in 1976.

The band included a breakdown of the costs of the record on the back of the record sleeve to inspire others to follow suit.

Following the Buzzcocks' lead, the Desperate Bicycles, another British band, formed for the sole "purpose of recording and releasing a single on their own label."[10] Vocalist Danny Wigley and keyboardist Nicky Stephens went into the studio to record their first two singles, "Smokescreen" and "Handlebars" in the spring of 1977. The songs took 3 hours to record and cost £153 (roughly $214), which included the cost of pressing 500 records and producing the sleeves. To cut costs, the band did not record a B-side; instead, it pressed the same songs on both sides of the record.

The band sold the singles to small record stores such as Small Wonder and Bonaparte Records and to various independent distributors such as Rough Trade, eventually selling out in four months. With their profits, the band turned around and pressed 1,000 more records, which sold out 2 weeks later. Despite their small success, the band never had the desire to sign with a record company. Wigley commented in the music magazine *New Musical Express* on Desperate Bicycles and their desire to remain independent: "For us it's really important to be independent. We've made a stand, small as it may be, and we've actually kept independent. *We're* in control of the music and of what we want to do."[11]

Self-Made Records

The success of the Buzzcocks and the Desperate Bicycles inspired many bands to go out and make their own records. According to writer Bob Stanley, between 1979 and 1981, there were roughly 900 DIY singles released. Most of the records had a similar look and were made in a similar way. The sleeves were often handmade photocopies of basic lettering or pictures. Photos of the band were rare. When they did grace a picture sleeve, the band was typically shown at a live show, emphasizing that the band was not a studio creation. Sometimes the photos were blurry or fuzzy to represent band unity by not highlighting actual faces or featuring any one member prominently.

Some of the sleeves were just simple brown paper bags with the names of the songs written in marker across the front. In many cases, the sleeves did not even list the full names of the band members. Rather than including a contact address for the band, it was much more common to list pressing plants, printers, and the costs of production calculated down to the last cent. By explaining how a record was made—sometimes with step-by-step instructions—it invited a much wider audience to

OAR FOLKJOKEOPUS

Independent record stores were one of the key elements of the growing indie music scene. They varied in their size and the kind of music they carried—some carried mainstream music along with more obscure music—but they provided an outlet for new music to be heard.

One successful indie record store that helped shape the indie music scene was located in Minneapolis, Minnesota. It was called Oar Folkjokeopus (partly named after an eccentric British folk album by Roy Harper called *Folkjokeopus*) and commonly referred to as Oar Folk. Owned by Vern Sanden, a record collector interested in rare and obscure music, the store became, according to the Twin/Tone label website, "a clubhouse for musical misfits of all kinds."[1]

Oar Folkjokeopus was the first store in the Midwest to carry hard-to-find imports and indie-label records well before the first punk explosion. The store became the cornerstone of the Minneapolis scene, and various independent club owners would inquire with the store before booking an up-and-coming band. Club owners would want to know what size crowd they should expect, what opening act to feature, and if they should book the show for more than one night. It was just one of the many intimate relationships that took place between artists, clubs, labels, and independent record stores.

1. Peter Jesperson, "The Twin/Tone Story," TwinTone.com, June 1998. www.twintone.com/story.html.

participate in making music. The DIY ethic stressed that artist and consumer were members of the same scene.

DIY Fanzines

The DIY ethic extended beyond recording into the realm of writing. Fans of the underground bands began making their own fan magazines, or fanzines, to follow the independent music scene. The fanzines were nonprofessional, often crude publications that included hand-printed text and collaged graphics. The publications were not funded by commercial or public ventures and were produced for minimal costs. Some of the most well-known fanzines at the time were *Sniffin' Glue*, *Sideburns*, *Jamming*, *London's Outrage*, and *Ugly Things*.

The fanzine *Sniffin' Glue* was started by Mark Perry in July 1976. Working as a bank clerk, Perry was inspired to start a fanzine after failing to find any mainstream publications that discussed punk bands such as the Ramones, who were

Punk fanzines were popular in the mid-1970s. Shown here is a collection of these DIY magazines.

touring England at the time. In a series of 12 issues over the course of a year, he chronicled various punk bands and concerts. In his first issue, Perry reviewed two Ramones shows in London as well as the exploits of other bands such as Blue Oyster Cult. Throughout the fanzine, Perry championed the DIY ethic.

The first issues of *Sniffin' Glue* only sold about 50 copies, but before the year was over, the circulation had increased to 15,000. Though the fanzine was popular among punk rockers, Perry feared that it would become popular in the mainstream and ceased publication after a single year.

In the first issue of fanzine *Sideburns*, which was created by Tony Moon in 1977, he included drawings of three chord patterns with the caption "This is a chord. This is another. This is a third. Now form

The Slits were a punk band comprised of all women who were signed by an indie label.

a band."[12] Similar messages such as these began showing up in several fanzines, and this DIY mentality encouraged others to create their own fanzines.

Start of Indie Labels

Independent record labels sprang up at the same time as fanzines. These labels helped bands record as well as distribute their music. Some of the more well-known indie record labels were Illegal, Deptford Fun City, Step Forward, Small Wonder, and Rough Trade. The latter was one of the most successful independent labels.

Rough Trade grew out of a successful record store of the same name in 1978. Founder Geoff Travis had an eclectic musical taste and signed a wide variety of bands, including Stiff Little Fingers, the Slits, Pere Ubu, Scritti Politti, and the Smiths.

Rough Trade was considered the most radical of the small labels. The label incorporated the idea of equality in all aspects of business, with the company being run like a co-op, which means that all workers received an equal amount of pay. Furthermore, it shunned all corporate business practices prevalent in the music industry. It avoided the glossy marketing campaigns that were common with the large labels and the 1970s rock bands they signed, such as Led Zeppelin and Pink Floyd. Rough Trade also did not rely on creating relationships with radio stations and large music retailers to create a fan base. Instead, it built relationships with musicians, independent record stores, and fanzines to gain exposure and sell music. Rough Trade showed that big budgets and expensive recording techniques were not necessary to sell a record, let alone record one. The label also worked to protect the artistic integrity of the musicians and did not compromise the artists' sound or intent in order to sell product.

As a small record label, Rough Trade also operated as an independent distributor. It helped bands that had recorded their own singles or albums secure a distribution channel, typically through a network of local, independently owned record shops. Rough Trade also signed contracts with bands on a record-by-record basis instead of forcing a band into a multi-album deal in which the pressures to produce product often meant a loss of creativity. Furthermore, all profits were split equally between the band and the label.

PUNK MAGAZINE

Punk magazine, which launched its first issue in January 1976, is the most lauded of all the punk fanzines. It was created by publisher Ged Dunn, cartoonist John Holmstrom, and "resident punk" Legs McNeil. Reporter Stephen MacLean described the magazine in an interview with Holmstrom and McNeil:

> Instead of the usual typeface, all the stories are hand lettered and it has the look of a comic book. Star reporter is Legs McNeil, who usually makes sure he asks the dumbest questions because punk, he says, is anti-intellectual … The magazine is nasty, it's honest, witty, and it's possibly the most original new publication to emerge since Australia's Oz *magazine became famous in the sixties.*[1]

This fanzine covered the New York underground music scene, mostly popularizing the punk rock scenes found at music clubs such as CBGB and Max's Kansas City. The fanzine released 15 issues; with its final issue in 1979. Its covers featured artists such as Iggy Pop, Blondie, Sex Pistols, Patti Smith, and Lou Reed.

1. "Flashez: Punk Magazine Interview (1977)," YouTube video, 4:56, posted by ABCLibrarySales, July 22, 2012. https://www.youtube.com/watch?v=R-1eTjat_Ps.

THE POWER OF DIY

Although many of these records were made for local distribution, copies of the records made their way through small underground music scenes in places such as Tokyo, Japan; Stockholm, Sweden; San Francisco; Los Angeles; and Washington, D.C. In 1978, *ZigZag* magazine cataloged 231 independent labels; this included large and small labels as well as a wide array of genres, including rock and roll, reggae, and punk. However, by 1980, the number had jumped to more than 800 due to the influx of punk labels.

DIY in America

The success of the independent British music scene inspired American youth to adopt a DIY mentality. As Britain's independent punk records made their way across the Atlantic, American youth saw that they, too, could record their own music without the help of a major record label.

In cities across America, such as Washington, D.C.; Minneapolis, Minnesota; and Los Angeles, small scenes were forming independently of one another, but all were influenced by the early American punk bands and the British punk scene. The music most associated with the American underground scene in the early 1980s was called hardcore. This music genre was a heavier, faster version of punk.

Following the British lead, local American bands and music fans created an extensive underground network that included college radio stations, fanzines, local cable-access shows, nightclubs, and independent record stores. Some of the more popular fanzines were *Punk* magazine, *Search & Destroy*, *Dry*, *Damage*, *New York Rocker*, *Rock Scene*, *Slash*, *Flipside*, *Maximumrocknroll*, and *Forced Exposure*, but there were hundreds of others, most of them photocopied and stapled together. The artwork that appeared in fanzines often consisted of photocopied collages with scrawled writing. Some of the record labels also featured such primitive images.

The earliest and most popular American indie record labels included SST, Dischord, Touch & Go, and Sub Pop, and these gained a large roster of artists. However, there were countless other labels that made significant contributions, including Alternative Tentacles, Taang!, Frontier, Slash, and Wax Trax. These labels built unique identities by creating particular aesthetics in their music, album art, and catalog copy.

Young people—mostly college students and social outcasts—were what allowed the scene to thrive. Small scenes in urban centers and college towns fostered unity among the like-minded. Young people wanted to see local bands and their friends' bands play rather than some of the popular mainstream acts.

Indie bands believed that it was easier to relate to the audience without the overblown gimmicks of mainstream rock acts. Author Michael Azerrad described the virtues of independent music:

> *Corporate rock was about living large; indie was about living realistically and being proud of it. Indie bands didn't need million-dollar promotional budgets and multiple costume changes. All they needed was to believe in themselves and for a few other people to believe in them, too. You didn't need some big corporation to fund you, or even verify that you were any good. It was about viewing as a virtue what most saw as a limitation.*[13]

This "virtue" became a badge of honor that drew more people to the independent scene.

Hardcore Labels

Since hardcore was never marketable to major labels, many bands chose to start their own record labels. Black Flag's Greg Ginn launched the first independent hardcore label, SST, when no other record company would listen to his band. When Ginn created SST, people became aware that there were other hardcore scenes in America. Until then, most bands thought that their local scene was the only place where they could hear or play hardcore music. Shortly after the

Black Flag released their debut album, Damaged, on their own independent record label, SST.

formation of SST, Minor Threat's Ian MacKaye created Dischord Records in Washington, D.C. These labels would become two of the defining indie labels in the 1980s.

SST and Dischord operated with a sense of community for their fellow hardcore musicians; however, they also ran their companies with a strong business sense. They sent album promos of their artists to rock critics, and they made sure that their artists were represented in the ads of all the major fanzines. Like many other independent labels, they signed bands on an album-by-album basis. That way, a band was not locked into three- or five-album contracts, and they had the freedom to change labels after each album.

The goal of Dischord was to allow bands to own their own music and not give up their rights or the money they earned to the big record companies. The label wanted the music to be accessible to as many people as possible. It limited the price of albums to $10, and concert tickets were often $5. Both Dischord and SST did not follow traditional music business practices. Instead, the labels operated out of necessity and learned as they went along. They made most of their decisions—such as pricing—based on their own identification with their audiences. They were young fans as well as entrepreneurs.

Blazing a New Trail

Touring was one of the ways hardcore bands could find interested listeners. Many of the early American hardcore bands created a touring path that would be copied by future indie rock bands as a standard way of promoting their music. College radio was in its infancy, so it was almost impossible for a punk or hardcore band to gain a national following unless it toured. Most big acts traditionally put out an album and then toured to promote it. However, hardcore bands often toured first and then put out a record.

Bands often worked together, sharing news of venues that welcomed hardcore music. Musicians would introduce each other to owners of venues, or all the bands from one record label might gain access to a certain club. Independent record labels would also support tours. By creating a network of partnerships, these early hardcore bands created a touring path across America. By the mid-1980s, there was an established pattern to making indie music: tour first, then record, and then release a record.

Hardcore Falls Apart

Initially, the hardcore scene was built on unity, and all the bands were very supportive of each other. Eventually, though, some of the small labels began to grow in size and become more

The Replacements started out by getting a lot of airplay as a punk band on college radio. However, they grew beyond their indie roots and are considered alternative rock pioneers.

considered those bands who signed with major labels to be sellouts. The indie movement split into factions, and the scene began to dissolve during the mid-1980s. According to Black Flag's Greg Ginn, hardcore fell apart when "people started seeing money in indy rock and … we couldn't go out on a limb anymore."[14]

Bands who remained with independent labels and refrained from signing with major labels kept the DIY aesthetic. The new shift in music in the mid-1980s to college radio heavily increased exposure for these bands. One change college radio brought was the addition of more diverse bands that introduced a range of music beyond the confines of just punk and hardcore.

popular. Indie bands such as Hüsker Dü and the Replacements also began getting airplay on college radio and grew beyond their indie roots. Many bands welcomed the attention and seized the opportunity to sign a recording contract with a larger label to obtain more money and increased publicity. Others in the scene

THE POWER OF DIY 37

CHAPTER THREE

Explosion of *College Rock*

College radio began in the middle-to-late 1980s as an alternative to mainstream radio. Mainstream radio provided listeners with Top 40 music with a lack of diversity in sound, whereas college radio played underground music. College radio stations played independent music, beyond the genres of just punk and hardcore that piqued the interest of those who wanted to hear more experimental music.

The addition of college radio was crucial in the development of alternative music because it exposed fans to independent music from across the nation. No longer did fans have to wait for new music that arrived via touring bands, such as in the early hardcore days; instead, they could hear new music from bands as soon as it was released. The music of bands who were played on college radio was eventually referred to as college rock since college radio was the main source of alternative music at the time.

College radio playlists moved beyond the punk and hardcore sounds that had characterized much of the independent music from the late 1970s and early 1980s and included a variety of music—from American bands such as Sonic Youth, the Pixies, and Dinosaur Jr. to British post-punk acts such as the Smiths, the Cure, and Siouxsie and the Banshees. The music played on college radio was part of a network of like-minded college students. No longer were these kids the disaffected youth of the punk and hardcore scene; they were educated, privileged, and had money to spend. However, like punk and hardcore, college rock was youth music that hinged upon audience identification; the bands and the fans were all part of the same circle. College rock narrowed the gap between the performer and audience and made the music seem more personal. Writer Hugo Lindgren described why he found college rock so appealing:

I was in college when the category

Rock band Sonic Youth formed in New York City in 1981. They have released many of their albums through independent labels, such as Neutral Records and SST Records.

known as "college rock" was popularized, and though it was as much a marketing [concept] as anything else, I bought the concept immediately. The Replacements and Hüsker Dü, the Blake Babies, the Pixies, and Pavement: These bands weren't just my idols, they felt like my peers, and a good part of the pleasure I took in their music was imagining that there wasn't much that separated me from them. Like the earliest punks, they made a virtue of their amateurism, of starting things without knowing where or how they'd end. And for someone like me, on the scary precipice of adulthood, that was an incredibly exciting fantasy: the notion that sheer guts, plus a willingness to bare your weaknesses (no vocal talent necessary!), could make you into a rock star.[15]

EXPLOSION OF COLLEGE ROCK

College radio became associated with independent or alternative music and greatly influenced the development of indie rock in the late 1990s. Most emerging indie rock musicians relied on college radio to gain exposure and build their fan bases. In fact, many indie rock bands became established via a network of college radio stations.

The Evolution of College Radio

Prior to the rise of college radio, most rock music fans listened to rock on commercial radio stations located on the FM spectrum. In the 1970s, commercial radio became a profitable market, with large music stations making considerable profits. Large corporations took notice of the booming market and started buying and creating new radio stations. By the mid-1980s, around 12,000 commercial stations competed for audiences. As a result, the market was incredibly fragmented, with each station playing to a small niche; soft hits, oldies, new rock, disco, and Latin music were some of the popular formats. During the mid-1980s, however, hard-rock music (played by bands such as Poison, Warrant, and Mötley Crüe) dominated the FM radio stations that played a "classic-rock" format.

Although there was no shortage of rock radio stations, most of the stations were playing the same music from the same bands. Many young music fans became increasingly bored with the hard-rock format and longed to hear new music with which they could identify. Many of these fans tuned in to local college radio stations to hear the alternative music that they could not hear on commercial radio. College radio stations offered an alternative to mainstream music, and most immersed in the college rock scene agreed: "The point is not to get lots of listeners. It's to support independent music, to give students experience in radio, and to expose those who care to [hear] music that they would have a hard time finding otherwise."[16]

College radio stations were located on college campuses and were operated and run by college students. The stations were mostly small, occupied a narrow bandwidth on the radio spectrum, and generally had low wattage. As a result, college stations did not have a great range, and most of the people tuning in were students. However, college radio exposed these local fans to underground music from around the country. People had an opportunity to hear bands that might not have played shows in their hometowns. Some of the earliest college radio stations that embraced alternative music were WXCI in Danbury, Connecticut; WPRB in Princeton, New Jersey; and Brown University's

WBRU in Providence, Rhode Island. WPRB disc jockey Jon Solomon had an alternative music show as early as 1986.

Most college stations operated with noncommercial licenses. This meant they had a lot of freedom to play whatever kind of music they wanted because they were not dependent on advertisers. Douglas Wolk, a former managing editor of *CMJ New Music Monthly*, explained why college radio stations had more freedom than commercial radio stations: "The most important thing about college radio stations is that they're not commercial—they don't need to run with ad sales in mind. College radio's mandate, then, is to provide programming that is thoughtful and daring."[17]

College radio introduced college students to underground bands such as the Pixies, the Cocteau Twins, and Neutral Milk Hotel. Many of these underground rock bands had been influenced by the punk bands of the 1970s and were experimental in their sound and songwriting. This appealed to the college music fans because it provided something new and an alternative to the classic rock music with which they had grown bored.

Cocteau Twins were an underground Scottish rock band whose experimental music appealed to college students. They were active for more than 20 years, disbanding in 1997.

EXPLOSION OF COLLEGE ROCK

THE PIXIES

One of college rock's most influential bands during the middle-to-late 1980s due to their willingness to experiment was the Pixies. The band formed in Boston, Massachusetts, in 1986 and included Black Francis and Kim Deal as dual singer-songwriters. Many bands at the time played a distinctive style of music that was easily classified as a certain musical genre. The Pixies, however, ignored musical classifications and

The Pixies were known for their experimental form of rock music.

Sound Experiments

In the mid-1980s, college rock broadened its sound beyond the hard-edged bands such as the Minutemen, Black Flag, and Minor Threat as bands began to experiment with new instruments. Some bands began to incorporate Casio keyboards, which could produce unique sounds that a guitar, bass, or drums could not. Other bands created a quieter guitar sound by decreasing the amount of distortion that typically had been used in the hardcore scene and by creating a more incorporated any number of musical styles into their songs. The band sometimes combined layered guitar distortion with simple folk rock harmonies or incorporated an experimental sound with dark rhythms.

Although critics liked the band, for most of their career, they received little airplay outside college radio. However, in Europe the band developed a huge following; just 18 months after their first rehearsal after a show in Germany, guitarist Joey Santiago "remembers a mob of fans attempting to pull him out of the door of the band's van by his feet."[1]

In 1989, the Pixies released *Doolittle* on a major label, and for a short time, they experienced some mainstream attention. Despite this, the band mostly remained in the underground circuit and toured successfully for a couple of years until they split up in 1991.

The band's popularity grew in the years after their break-up, and they inspired bands such as Nirvana and Radiohead. Kurt Cobain claimed the song "Smells Like Teen Spirit" was his attempt to sound like the Pixies, and Radiohead refused to play following the Pixies. "The Pixies opening for us is like The Beatles opening for us. I won't allow it. There's no way we can follow the Pixies,"[2] said Radiohead frontman Thom Yorke regarding the Pixies' 2004 Coachella set, which was part of the band's reunion tour that year. The band remained together until Deal's departure in 2013. Deal was replaced by the Muffs' Kim Shattuck, who was fired just a few months into the band's tour that same year. Shattuck was replaced by Paz Lenchantin. In 2014, the Pixies released *Indie Cindy*, which was followed by *Head Carrier* in 2016.

1. Alexi Petridis, "Interview: Pixies: 'We Were Off the Planet,'" *The Guardian*, November 21, 2013. www.theguardian.com/music/2013/nov/21/pixies-we-were-off-plant-black-francis.

2. Quoted in John Mendelssohn, *Gigantic: The Story Of Frank Black and The Pixies*. London, UK: Omnibus Press, 2004, p. 197.

melodic pop sound. Some bands even began to embrace some traditionally mainstream rock practices because it was an alternative to some of the conventions becoming established in punk and hardcore. For example, Massachusetts bands such as Dinosaur Jr. and Sebadoh often incorporated extended guitar solos and rising melodies, which were components that punks had rejected earlier.

In addition to experimenting with sound, many bands began to focus on lyrics. The lyrics of many college rock bands often referred

EXPLOSION OF COLLEGE ROCK

JOHN PEEL'S SUPPORT OF INDIE MUSIC

Throughout radio's history, numerous radio disc jockeys (DJs) have single-handedly changed the careers of various alternative rock bands and musicians by playing their music on the radio. One of the most respected and longest-lasting was British DJ and broadcaster John Peel. Beginning in 1967, Peel hosted a show on Radio 1, the new pop music station for the British Broadcasting Corporation (BBC). He soon became a popular fixture, and thousands of listeners tuned in to hear his shows.

One of his trademarks was the development of the John Peel Sessions. These sessions included performances by bands who prerecorded four songs at the BBC's studios, which were then exclusively played on Peel's show. He had an eclectic and avant-garde taste in music and showcased new music to his listeners. He became a strong advocate of the punk rock movement and other independent music that followed. Peel's support helped launch the careers of several indie musicians during the 1980s, including the Cure, the Wedding Present, and the Smiths.

Peel's Radio 1 show lasted 37 years and ended with his death in 2004. More than 2,000 artists had recorded 4,000 sessions with him over the years.

---

to art, literature, and philosophy—topics many artists had studied in college. For instance, the college rock band R.E.M. from Athens, Georgia, wrote obscure lyrics tinted with artistic references. Other bands wrote introspective lyrics (though many of the early hardcore bands would consider themselves introspective) that questioned themselves on a personal level instead of questioning society, as many punks had.

The most popular of the college rock bands were the Replacements, R.E.M., the Smiths, and Dinosaur Jr. However, college rock also embraced some mainstream acts, including U2, Peter Gabriel, and Sting. They were considered part of the college rock genre because they wrote songs about social issues, which appealed to many students on college campuses.

Indie Bands Land on Music Charts

At first, college rock had a mostly underground following of students interested in independent music. The music began to gain momentum, however, as these college rock bands traveled through college rock towns. Many of the students who worked at the college radio stations naturally attended a lot of shows and were constantly exposed to new music. In turn, they would play

The Smiths formed in 1982 and quickly became known for their gloomy lyrics.

these bands on their radio shows. The record industry soon began to take notice of the small successes independent bands were having on college radio.

One of the reasons why the record industry began to pay attention to college rock was because it was the first independent music to make ripples on the music charts. Two bands who helped bring independent music onto the music charts were New Order and the Smiths. The Smiths, known for their gloomy lyrics and downbeat pop sound, were a British band who had much success on the record charts despite being signed to an independent label. They were signed to Rough Trade, and their 1984 self-titled debut entered the UK charts at number 2. Their song "Heaven Knows I'm Miserable Now" reached number 10 on the UK singles charts. The band's second album, *Meat Is Murder*, landed at the top of the UK charts within the first week of its release. These chart successes brought some mainstream attention to the variety of music that was escaping major label notice.

CASSETTE TAPES

One of the offshoots of the DIY ethic of punk that occurred at the same time that college rock was in full swing was the home recording of compact audiocassettes. Bands often recorded themselves on tape at home and then passed the tapes on to friends or distributed them through independent labels. The tapes were also sold via mail order or were exchanged in a loose network of independent labels and fanzines. Some bands would copy their music after being sent a blank tape and a self-addressed envelope. It was a popular way for indie musicians to distribute their music.

The cassette-tape movement was first popular in Britain during the post-punk period from 1978 to 1984. In the United States, however, the trend occurred during the middle-to-late 1980s (and even into the 1990s), after *New Musical Express*, a weekly UK music magazine, released a compilation called *C86* in 1986. The compilation was released on cassette tape and was available through mail order. It included bands such as Primal Scream, the Bodines, and the Pastels.

songs. For instance, singer Michael Stipe was known for mumbling hard-to-understand lyrics. Once R.E.M. became more visible, Stipe wondered if the band should adjust their sound to satisfy their new audience. He explained in a 1987 interview, "There's a little more weight on my shoulders as far as what I say ... I guess I've figured out that I can't just blabber anything I want to anymore, which I've done before, though not a great deal. On some of the earlier songs, whatever I happened to be singing, we recorded it."[18]

Many bands, including R.E.M., experienced the problems that resulted from the crossover success of alternative rock in the mainstream pop world—a problem that exists for some artists even today. When a band reaches the mainstream, they have a much larger audience. Original fans of the band feel less special if they are one of thousands of listeners. Some of these fans accuse the band of selling out and surrendering their indie credentials. This set of fans believes indie bands lose their integrity and often their authenticity if they try to please mass audiences.

Lou Barlow, lead singer of one of the quintessential college rock bands, Sebadoh, commented on abandoning the band's "indie cred" to simply play music. Instead, Barlow stated that he wants their music to reach more than a fanzine editor who gets upset when their favorite band goes mainstream:

It seems like a misnomer. It's not really important to us, and we're not going to cater to people's personal politics ... If you record and put something out, you should be prepared for the idea that maybe more than one person will wanna listen to it. And then you have to accept the fact that that could be a million or two million. Or whatever. It's all the same to me.[19]

College radio remained a helpful medium for unknown bands to gain exposure, regardless of whether a band remained popular on the indie circuit or made it to the mainstream. While college towns embraced their local bands, many of the most popular bands began to enter the mainstream circuit. As time went on, the music of 1980s college rock faded into the background, and a new genre of alternative rock music replaced it.

CHAPTER FOUR

The Emergence of Grunge Music

Various genres of alternative music have remained a product of underground music scenes throughout history and would eventually lead to the creation of indie rock. However, a few college rock bands managed to break out from the mold and find commercial success with major labels. As this phase of music inevitably began to dissolve, a new music scene emerged from Washington State thanks to a band not affiliated with the college scene, but with a dreary city about 2 hours outside of Seattle—this band was called Nirvana.

In the early 1990s, Nirvana would forever break down the barrier between alternative and mainstream when their album *Nevermind* was released. The album's first single, "Smells Like Teen Spirit," had a brash yet melodic guitar sound coupled with lyrics about youth culture, and it was an escape for bored teenagers and 20-year-olds. "Smells Like Teen Spirit" also had its own video, which was made on a small budget and displayed a band without makeup, special effects, or gimmicks. The video brought instant attention to Nirvana, and they received what seemed like overnight success across America.

The success of Nirvana drew attention to their home state of Washington, where several other bands seemed to be playing a similar sound and sporting a similar non–rock star appearance. Emphasizing the hard-rock sound and disheveled look of the bands, critics called the music and the scene "grunge."

Grunge soon dominated the airwaves, and many of these alternative bands that were used to playing small venues in front of friends were suddenly embarking on major tours, playing in front of larger audiences, and being signed by major labels. Like all scenes,

Nirvana became one of the most successful grunge bands. They released their debut album Bleach *in 1989.*

grunge was quickly co-opted and sold, becoming more of a marketing term used to sell youth culture to the masses than a distinct genre of music. Major labels had finally figured out how to cash in on alternative culture.

Secluded Music Scene

Around 1985, an alternative music scene was starting to take root in the Seattle area, including Aberdeen, an isolated logging town located midway up the Pacific coast in Washington State. Aberdeen was a depressed town economically, especially after automation in the logging industry had created a high rate of unemployment. According to Kurt Cobain, former lead singer and guitarist for Nirvana, Aberdeen was "totally secluded from any culture at all."[20]

Aberdeen, like Seattle, experiences heavy rainfall most of the year. As a result, people typically stayed inside, and the area youth often chose to play music to eliminate boredom. Cobain described

THE EMERGENCE OF GRUNGE MUSIC   51

how he created his own punk music since such music was not accessible in Aberdeen:

> *The Sex Pistols, the Buzzcocks, any 'seventy-seven [1977] punk rock band was totally influential to our music. But it was almost impossible to get exposed to English punk. We only had one radio station, a soft rock AM station. I remember being about fourteen and having a subscription to* Creem *magazine and I would read about the Sex Pistols, but I never got to hear anything ... I decided to create my own punk rock with my electric guitar.*[21]

At that time, there was not much of a live music scene in Washington. Seattle was not a town through which bands toured—most bands went only as far north as San Francisco. However, there were venues to hear live local music, including the Showbox and the Gorilla Gardens. If a band wanted to put on a show, band members would do all the work themselves—rent a hall, take tickets, and even clean up afterward.

Bands were not typically concerned with success in Seattle. They were mostly interested in playing music for their friends. According to record producer Jack Endino, "Nobody was too worried about success because we were living in Seattle. It wasn't LA [Los Angeles]. Nobody was gonna come sign us."[22]

A Unique Sound

There was a defining quality that characterized most of the music being created in Seattle. Many bands were influenced by the punk rock and hardcore music of the early 1980s bands, as well as classic hard-rock bands such as Aerosmith. These garage bands reinvented punk by adding incredible amounts of guitar distortion to make a "fuzzy" sound. The sound was then amplified to incredibly high decibels and was mixed with plenty of feedback. It was what one *Newsweek* writer once termed "a wall of white noise."[23] Guns N' Roses bass player Duff McKagan described the sound that came from Seattle: "You gotta understand Seattle ... It's *grungy*. People are into rock & roll and into noise, and they're building airplanes all the time, and there's a lot of noise, and there's rain and musty garages. Musty garages create a certain noise."[24]

The Seattle bands also believed in recording their music as if they were playing a live show. In polished studio recordings, it is possible for bands to create a richer sound by overlaying tracks on top of one another—sometimes as many as 24 tracks. The sound from each track is then separated, edited, and then put back together (otherwise known as remastering). These techniques are often used to create a rich tone and range. However, a band cannot replicate this sound at a live show. Seattle bands avoided these recording tricks, preferring that their recordings mimic their live shows. Mudhoney, a successful band from Seattle, chose to record an album on cheap four-track equipment, despite having the means to rent a nice studio with multitrack recorders that could clean up any performance.

Sub Pop

In the late 1980s, most Seattle bands did not expect to gain the attention of major record labels—that happened in Los Angeles or New York. However, a well-known independent record label named Sub Pop (which had started out as a fanzine called *Subterranean Pop* in 1980) decided to harness the Seattle sound and promote it as best it could. In 1988, Sub Pop Records released a box set called *Sub Pop 200*. It contained bands such as Soundgarden, Mudhoney, and Nirvana, all of whom went on to become influential bands in the 1990s. The set was also sold with a 20-page booklet filled with photographs capturing long-haired band members wearing flannel shirts, dripping in sweat, and frantically playing their guitars. The booklet was responsible for making that image—especially the flannel shirts and unkempt hair—the image of the grunge scene.

Sub Pop went on to record many of Seattle's grunge bands and was the independent record label of choice for many like-minded bands looking to record an album. Nirvana, formed in 1987 by high school friends Kurt Cobain and Krist Novoselic, recorded their first album, *Bleach*, on Sub Pop in 1989 for roughly $600. Nirvana went on to record their next album, *Nevermind*, with Sub Pop in 1991, even signing a contract with the label. Many local music fans turned to Sub Pop recordings to hear new music. Quite a few bands gained modest followings after appearing on the Sub Pop label.

Despite the small successes of local bands, Sup Pop was not a very stable business and was close to bankruptcy in 1991. Label owners Jonathan Poneman and Bruce Pavitt decided to sell 49 percent interest in the label to Warner Bros.'s Geffen Records for $20 million. (The label was originally a $20,000 investment.) This included the buyout of the remainder of Nirvana's contract with Sub Pop. Poneman and Pavitt were to maintain complete artistic control of the label and would receive 2 percent of the royalties Geffen earned from Nirvana's *Nevermind* album. Following the partial buyout, Geffen went on to market the band with an intensity that underground music had not previously experienced. The label unleashed massive quantities of radio promos to college

HI, HOW ARE YOU

Singer-songwriter Daniel Johnston is the perfect example of the complex relationship between creating indie music while also desiring fame and success. Born in Sacramento, California, in 1961, Johnston has been an artist, filmmaker, and singer-songwriter since his early teens. From a young age, he made music in the hope of one day becoming famous. He originally

Daniel Johnston is a singer-songwriter who suffers from bipolar disorder. He has inspired many musicians and songwriters.

radio station managers. The band also made the video for their song "Smells Like Teen Spirit," which was placed in heavy rotation on MTV. As a result, Nirvana received much airplay and consequently became a nationally recognized name on college radio.

Grunge Reigns Supreme

Nirvana's album *Nevermind* was released in September 1991 and went gold in a few weeks. When the video for "Smells Like Teen Spirit" appeared in October 1991, it was not long before the band was selling out clubs across the country. By mid-January 1992, *Nevermind* was the number-1 album in the United States. It bumped Michael Jackson out of the number-1 spot on Billboard's album charts.

As "Smells Like Teen Spirit" leaped immediately into the mainstream markets, major labels looked to sign any Seattle band they could. Record executives flocked to the city, as did bands hoping to capitalize on the music scene.

played piano but then switched to guitar after he moved to Austin, Texas. It was at about this time that he began exhibiting signs of bipolar disorder.

Johnston began his career as an independent musician by recording his music on cassettes in his garage using a $59 Sanyo boombox. He dubbed each tape individually and handcrafted the covers for each cassette by pasting his personal cartoon drawings to the cassette cover. Johnston would then distribute his tapes by hand to newspaper writers, club owners, or anyone who would accept one of them. Johnston eventually played some shows in Austin and gained a cult following by those who were intrigued by his odd behavior but clever and unusual lyrics. Even Nirvana's Kurt Cobain was drawn to his music and was seen wearing a T-shirt featuring the artwork from Johnston's 1983 album, *Hi, How Are You*.

In 1994, Johnston signed with Atlantic Records but was dropped by the major label when his album sold poorly. Despite his mainstream failure, he has been a favorite of underground music bands. Close to 200 artists, including Pearl Jam, have recorded covers of his songs. In July 2017, Johnston announced he would be retiring from live performance. However, he embarked on one last North American tour in the fall of that year supported by artists who were influenced by his music, such as the Preservation All-Stars, the Districts, Modern Baseball, Jeff Tweedy, and Built to Spill.

Because Nirvana had been such a success on college radio, record executives sought out Seattle bands played on college radio stations, hoping to cash in on the next Nirvana. Like all successful scenes, grunge was soon seen as a commodity and sold as a trendy alternative to pop music. No longer was the emphasis on the music but rather on the look and laid-back atmosphere of grunge. Movies such as Cameron Crowe's 1992 film *Singles* tried to replicate the Seattle music scene, and high-end clothing designers marketed designs that mimicked the clothes of many of the Seattle musicians. Grunge bands appeared on the covers of mainstream music magazines such as *Rolling Stone*. A 1992 cover of the magazine featured Nirvana with the headline "New Faces of Rock."

Nirvana and a number of other Seattle bands dominated the mainstream radio charts for the next five years. Bands such as Soundgarden, Pearl Jam, Alice in Chains, Screaming Trees, and Mudhoney not only ushered in a new sound but also

RISE OF THE RIOT GRRRL

The Riot Grrrl movement sprouted in the early 1990s as a response to the male-dominated grunge music scene. It was loud, fast, and angry-sounding rock music played by women. Riot Grrrl music focused on anger and aggressiveness rather than girly cuteness or innocence. It was started by a group of women in Washington, D.C., and Olympia, Washington, who were calling for a feminist revolution in rock music. The slogan that captured their philosophy was "Revolution Girl Style Now."[1]

Bands such as Bratmobile and Bikini Kill were at the forefront of the movement that advocated for all-female bands and female ownership of record labels. Jenny Toomey of the band

Sleater-Kinney (shown here with former drummer Toni Gogin, center) was inspired by Riot Grrrl bands such as Bikini Kill.

swept aside the pop mainstream. By 1994, the seven best-selling Seattle bands generated $200 million in gross revenues for their major labels. The grunge scene (which also came to embrace bands outside of Seattle that had a similar sound) dominated MTV and some music charts. Grunge was no longer a local outsider scene; it was a defining fixture of the mainstream music industry.

Not everyone was thrilled about the success of grunge music. Most of the bands had no idea how the mainstream music industry worked, and many were surprised at the level of fame that came along with signing with a major label. Bassist Kim Thayil of Soundgarden said,

Kinda figured we'd play guitar or drums ... sing ... make a record, play a show. People like your

INDIE ROCK: FINDING AN INDEPENDENT VOICE

Tsunami was one participant who took the movement seriously. After becoming frustrated with the mainstream recording industry, Toomey, along with friend Kristen Thompson, formed the record label called Simple Machines.

The twosome advocated a DIY ethic and encouraged women and all independent musicians to be in control of their own businesses. They even wrote and produced a 24-page manual that described the exact process for recording and distributing music independently. The Riot Grrrl movement reached its peak in 1992 and 1993.

One band deeply influenced by the Riot Grrrl movement was Sleater-Kinney, who have been recognized as "America's best rock band"[2] by *TIME* magazine's Greil Marcus and "America's best punk band ever,"[3] by Rolling Stone's Rob Sheffield. The all-female trio from Olympia is currently comprised of Corin Tucker, Carrie Brownstein, and Janet Weiss. Before forming Sleater-Kinney in 1994, Tucker had played in the Riot Grrrl band Heavens to Betsy and Brownstein in the punk rock band Excuse 17. The band released seven albums up until 2007, including *Dig Me Out*, which is recognized as their breakthrough album that earned them more exposure to the masses. Between 2007 and 2013, the band went on hiatus; however, in 2015, the band returned with their eighth studio album, *No Cities to Love*.

1. Vice Staff, "How the Spice Girls Ripped 'Girl Power' from Its Radical Roots," *Vice*, November 4, 2016. www.vice.com/en_us/article/bn3vq5/girl-power-spice-girls-jenny-stevens-geri-horner.

2. Quoted in "About," Sleater-Kinney, accessed on May 17, 2018. www.sleater-kinney.com/about/.

3. Quoted in "About," Sleater-Kinney.

---

record, and they like your show … [We] couldn't really anticipate it becoming interviews, videos and photo sessions. In the forefront of our minds we sort of knew that these were things that went along with the job but you never really can anticipate it until you are there. We can do without the fame stuff.[25]

The mainstream success of grunge music changed the underground music scene and made it difficult for any alternative band to exist outside of the spotlight. Singer and guitarist Eric Bachmann of Archers of Loaf claimed, "It made it impossible for there to be any sort of an underground scene. The minute a band put out a single, the major labels knew about it. People who were doing dishes really hated being poor, so they took a chance, signed to a label and got dropped a year later."[26]

Downsides of the Music Industry

The music recording industry is not like other businesses. Major labels lose money on 9 out of 10 records, meaning they have a 90 percent failure rate. With one hit record, they must cover the costs for running the rest of their business. As a result, record label executives invest a lot of money into bands that they think might succeed, but if success is not forthcoming, the label is likely to temper its support or drop the band altogether. Many bands are also told that when they sign a record deal, they will keep some artistic control. The reality, however, is that the record label will ultimately determine what single will be released, if it releases any at all. When such string pulling occurs, many bands feel that the record labels are responsible for the demise of their careers.

The Dandy Warhols, a band that signed with Capitol Records in 1996,

The Dandy Warhols have released the majority of their albums with independent record labels.

INDIE ROCK: FINDING AN INDEPENDENT VOICE

have disagreed with the way major labels handle their artists. Lead singer Courtney Taylor-Taylor believes that the reason indie music reestablished itself in the late 1990s was because more and more bands had negative experiences—such as lack of promotion—with the major labels. For example, although Capitol spent $400,000 on a music video for the Dandy Warhols shortly after signing the band, company executives quickly changed their minds about promoting the band and never released the video. Because the band had signed a contract, they could not look to another label to help promote their music, despite being ignored by their label. Taylor-Taylor said,

> Indie rock happened because of this, you know, because of what we have experienced being on a major label, what every major label says won't happen to you. They won't tell you what single to put out, they won't take your pop song. That's just bad advertising for the band ... If I'd only been just a little bit smarter.[27]

Return to the Underground

Once grunge music had entered into the mainstream, many musicians and labels retreated to the underground as a way of protesting the major-label music structure and the supposed selling out of alternative music. Some believed that to remain truly independent, they had to avoid the mainstream music industry entirely. The lead singer of Beat Happening, Calvin Johnson, and Candice Pedersen went on to form indie label K Records, which produced early releases from Beck, Modest Mouse, and Built to Spill. Other labels with similar agendas formed in resistance to the typical grunge sound, including Kill Rock Stars, which produced early albums from Elliott Smith, Sleater-Kinney, and the Decemberists.

Lead singer and guitarist Mac McCaughan of popular college-rock band Superchunk was courted by major labels but refused to sign with them. Instead, he and fellow bandmate Laura Ballance formed Merge Records, which would remain one of the more well-known and successful independent labels. Merge was modeled on the idea that even selling a few thousand records could earn both the band and the label some money.

Many independent labels were able to offer bands a much greater chance at success on their own terms. A band might not become rich, but it might be able to sell a few thousand records and keep a much larger portion of the profits than if the band was signed to a major label. Corey Rusk, the founder of independent label Touch and Go, operated his business on the honor system, using verbal agreements instead of written contracts muddled with legal writing. Rusk always paid bands 50 percent of the net profits of their records, which is 4 times the standard royalty rate in the corporate music industry. Although the label did not offer huge advances like the major labels, the profit-split system was in some cases better financially for bands. For example, an album that sells 50,000 records might earn a band more money in the long run than if they had signed up for a large advance and a smaller percent of net sales. In return for the profit-split, Touch and Go had the right to press the records as the market demanded them.

The Brian Jonestown Massacre

Some bands went to extremes to remain independent and outside of the record industry. The Brian Jonestown Massacre, a band that was playing what some critics called postmodern 1960s revivalist music, adamantly believed that to stay true to their artistic intentions, they had to resist the pressures of the corporate music industry. The band, who played small venues with sometimes just a handful of people in the audience, could record as much music as they wanted on the independent Bomp! label. For instance, in 1996, the band produced three full-length albums. According to lead singer Anton Newcombe, it cost only around $17 to record the album *Thank God for Mental Illness*. Newcombe once commented on the desire to sell his music for a profit: "I'm not for sale ... The Beatles were for sale, I give it [music] away."[28]

The Brian Jonestown Massacre was still able to gain fans by remaining independent. The band was able to make records without a major record deal, and its members were able to tour. They also landed on magazine covers despite not having the backing of the corporate music industry. There were several artists who preferred to make music this way. Some, however, would question the merits of remaining truly independent.

Some bands were often broke and had no real homes. Sometimes they lived with friends; other times they traded their music for a house to live in and food to eat. Many indie bands that chose to tour on their own often found themselves in these situations. Some bands worked regular jobs in order to make a living and played their music on the side.

Carlo McCormick of *Paper*, a magazine devoted to pop culture, described the difficulty Newcombe faced making a living as a musician while also adhering to his artistic principle of not selling out: "He thinks success and credibility are

IN PROTEST OF MAJOR LABELS

The first indie music was partly a rebellion against the way major record labels conducted business. In recent years, even bands and artists that have found success on major labels have started speaking out against the record industry. Courtney Love, lead singer of the popular 1990s alternative rock group Hole, described why she believes record companies take advantage of artists in their business practices:

> Record companies have a 3% success rate. That means that 3% of all records released by major labels go gold or platinum. How do record companies get away with a 97% failure rate that would be totally unacceptable in any other business?
>
> Record companies keep almost all the profits. Recording artists get paid a tiny fraction of the money earned by their music. That allows record executives to be incredibly sloppy in running their companies and still create enormous amounts of cash for the corporations that own them.[1]

1. Courtney Love and Johnny Temple, "On the Record: Toward a Union Label," *The Nation*, September 6, 2001. www.thenation.com/article/record-toward-union-label/.

Courtney Love was the lead singer of the 1990s band Hole. She was also married to Nirvana's Kurt Cobain.

THE EMERGENCE OF GRUNGE MUSIC 61

mutually exclusive terms, which is an easy bag to inherit, but a difficult one to haul through every decision of your career because as a musician you want to reach the biggest possible audience and as an artist you want to impact culture in the deepest way possible."[29]

The Next Music Discovery

The success of grunge forever changed the nature of how new music was heard. After grunge had run its course in the mainstream, record executives, recognizing the power of youth music, again turned to the underground music scene in search of new music. In fact, in 1996, many critics predicted another underground music explosion. There were several highly anticipated albums released in 1996 by Sebadoh, Guided By Voices, and Archers of Loaf. However, these bands, popular in the college-rock radio circuit, were not yet recognized by the mainstream, which was still dominated by grunge and hard-rock bands. In the next few years, these bands emerged into the spotlight as a new rock genre was born: indie rock.

CHAPTER FIVE

Indie Rock
Is Born

Indie rock initially was the alternative music of college kids in the late 1990s. After the grunge scene began to fade, music shifted away from the pounding drums, grinding electric guitars, and screaming vocals of grunge music. Bands began to incorporate softer qualities that had been prominent in tamer college rock music. The music became more literate and included stimulating topics with thought-provoking and introspective song lyrics. For instance, the lyrics of indie rock band Bright Eyes focus on topics such as the nature of existence and death. Wilco lead singer Jeff Tweedy's lyrics explore the various psychological states of the human mind. With more thoughtful lyrics came more melodic song structures that fit the mood better than distorted guitar riffs.

Although independent rock music has been made for decades, record labels and corporate executives hatched the term "indie rock" to represent the "new" alternative music market in their advertising and marketing campaigns. Although there were plenty of indie rock bands in the late 1990s, it was not until the 2000s that the term "indie rock" reached the mainstream. In November 2004, indie rock poster boy Conor Oberst claimed the two top spots on the singles charts. By 2005, Death Cab for Cutie debuted at number 4 on the Billboard 200 with their record *Plans*.

The success of independent record labels is mostly because indie rock has been marketed and promoted as the next youth music. Indie rock bands can be heard in commercials and popular television shows and seen on MTV. Furthermore, there are countless subgenres of music that all fall under the indie rock umbrella, bringing even more attention to the scene. Indie music festivals have become ideal places to hear the newest music. Being "indie" is not adhering to a specific style of music; instead, it is embracing the spirit, integrity, and youthful energy of

Conor Oberst founded his indie rock project Bright Eyes in 1995.

are creating divisions within themselves that operate similar to indie labels. As a result, the boundary between what constitutes independent music and corporate music is unclear. No longer do independent labels and major labels seem to be on opposing teams. While some artists and labels in the movement retain a DIY ethic and independent spirit, that mentality means something different than it did in the days of early punk and hardcore. Many critics wonder if the indie rock scene will fade out like grunge or whether it will survive far into the 21st century.

making music that supposedly tries hard not to compromise artistic goals for corporate sponsorship.

The popularity of indie rock and indie labels is reshaping the recording industry. Major labels are recognizing the benefits of operating their labels more like independent ones. Some big labels are buying out indie labels but keeping the business structure intact to continue the successful model. Other major labels

DIY Makes a Comeback

The popularity of indie rock has increased thanks to advances in technology that have allowed greater numbers of artists to produce music on an independent label. Therefore, at the same time that the genre was being orchestrated, in part by major labels, there was also some sense of DIY that remained.

In the early 1990s, when CDs were becoming increasingly popular, they were expensive to produce if a band was interested in pressing less than 5,000 CDs. The setup costs and minimum-run requirements kept many bands from making their own CDs. By the mid-1990s, however, many more independent manufacturers were available to bands. Some of these smaller manufacturers would do runs of less than 1,000 CDs and charge roughly $1 per unit. Some bands even shared the costs by creating split CDs with other bands.

There were also several independent recording studios available to musicians. Record producer Steve Albini built his own recording studio to serve independent musicians. He worked on a sliding payment scale and sometimes offered bands his services for free. He also worked to demystify the process of making CDs. On Shellac's 1994 album *At Action Park*, a CD he produced, the sleeve stated, "This was not mastered directly to metal or pressed into 165 grams of virgin dye-blackened vinyl. There is, in fact, nothing at all special about the manufacture of this compact disc."[30]

As technology became more sophisticated, more bands began to record themselves in home studios. With a computer and a CD burner, any band could record their music onto a CD. Many bands then passed out their homemade CDs at shows. This became standard practice for any band starting out, and it allowed the band complete control over the distribution of their music.

Emo Emerges

Another reason that indie rock has been so far-reaching is that the genre encompasses a wide array of subgenres. Many of these subgenres started in small scenes and have been marketed to audiences as being a very specialized music. Some of these newer categories include post-rock, ambient, shoegaze, slowcore, nu gaze, noise rock, post-punk revival, sadcore, math rock, and emo.

One of the offshoots of indie rock that gained a lot of attention in the 1990s and early 21st century—and has contributed to the overall popularity of indie rock—is emo. As they did with the term indie rock, many record companies appropriated the term emo as a marketing tool to sell albums. Emo is short for "emotional music" and, like indie rock, is difficult to define. This is due to the fact that musicians often do not want to be labeled emo because it locks them into a particular category of music—one that is often dismissed by a lot of musicians and critics as overly weepy and self-indulgent. Author Jim DeRogatis disagrees with that description: "I prefer to think of it as punk rock that's more melodic and introspective/depressing than

The Vans Warped Tour helped launch Fall Out Boy's career in the early 2000s.

hardcore, but still tapping into that primal energy and anger."[31]

Some well-known emo bands include Dashboard Confessional, Jimmy Eat World, Taking Back Sunday, Fall Out Boy, Brand New, Paramore, and the Used. One music festival that showcased several emo bands during the genre's heyday was the *Vans Warped Tour*, which launched in 1995 and celebrated its last touring year in 2018. The annual festival was the longest running North American touring music festival and appealed to fans of several genres of music, including punk, pop, hip-hop, indie rock, ska, alternative rock, and more. Kevin Lyman, founder of the festival, expressed his appreciation for getting to work with countless bands over the years: "I am so grateful to have worked with more than 1,700 bands over the last 23 summers. I wish I could thank every band that has played the tour."[32]

Annual Music Festivals

While the *Vans Warped Tour* brought exposure for many emo bands, other music festivals across the country helped spread the word,

FUELED BY RAMEN

Record label Fueled By Ramen was one independent record label that helped support the emo scene. The label was started by John Janick in his dorm room at the University of Florida in 1996, as he teamed up with Less Than Jake drummer Vinnie Fiorello. The label began releasing limited edition 7-inch (17.78 cm) singles, along with full-length releases from indie bands, such as the Hippos and the Impossibles. Janick explained his motivations for starting the label: "We were really passionate about the independent rock scene, but record labels didn't really seem to be taking notice of what was happening in it ... We said, 'We like these bands, these bands all work hard, why not try and get this music out to people?'"[1]

The label released Jimmy Eat World's self-titled EP in 1998, which served as the band's breakthrough. That same year, the label set up its own office. In 2002, the label achieved more success when it released Yellowcard's *The Underdog* EP, and the next year, it released Fall Out Boy's debut album *Take This To Your Grave*. "Our job is to help bands get their creative vision out there," Janick said. "We try to be involved in every step of the process in order to help them express their vision and make sure that we can get that across to the fans."[2]

1. Quoted in "Fueled By Ramen," Fueled By Ramen Records, Press Release, accessed on May 17, 2018. fueledbyramen.com/press/fueledbyramen/fueledbyramen.bio.pdf.

2. Quoted in "Fueled By Ramen," Fueled By Ramen Records, Press Release.

popularizing the indie rock genre—and its many subgenres. There are several American festivals that take place each year to showcase indie bands. Some of the most recognizable have been *North by Northwest* in Portland, Oregon; *South by Southwest* in Austin, Texas; and the *College Media Journal (CMJ) Music Marathon* in New York City. However, both the *North by Northwest* and *CMJ* festivals are no longer occurring.

The *CMJ* festival was originally created in 1980 to help bring together college radio stations from across the country. It was an important avenue for independent record labels to get exposure and for college radio stations to discover new music. At the 2004 festival, the unknown Canadian indie rock band Arcade Fire gained exposure after playing several small shows during the weeklong festival. Shortly after appearing at the festival, they released their critically acclaimed album *Funeral* on the indie label Merge. The exposure at the festival created a small fan base that bought the album. The band gained a large following in a short amount of time, due to word of mouth and radio airplay. The band headlined the festival the following year, where more than 1,000 bands converged to perform in New York City. Well-established indie rock acts such as the New Pornographers, who occupied the top spot on *CMJ*'s college-radio chart, played sold-out shows.

Though the larger indie festivals were initially started to feature independent musicians, over the years, they have become so popular that critics fear the events are no longer about connecting new bands with interested audiences. For instance, *South by Southwest* has become what some observers consider a spring break destination catering to a party crowd and not appreciative fans. Some of the larger festivals also show signs of corporate influences because advertising has become a key component in the success of the festivals. Many festivals are also intermixing musical venues with panels, display booths, and keynote speakers. The number of artists and the various added attractions only serve to raise the admission costs, which can be hundreds of dollars.

Indie rockers Arcade Fire won the Grammy Award for Album of the Year in 2011.

As alternatives to the larger indie festivals, local festivals are cropping up in cities across America. Many of the people promoting these festivals are interested in providing lesser-known and local bands with an opportunity to play in a festival environment. San Francisco is one city that has embraced an annual indie music festival called *Noise Pop*. The festival lasts for several days and takes place at various music venues. The aim of *Noise Pop* is to offer intimate settings for music lovers to see bands inexpensively. In addition, it allows independent bands to hear their peers play. Festival founder Kevin Arnold works hard to keep the festival from becoming a "record label schmooze fest." Arnold stated, "They have to realize that I am not booking tons of shows of unsigned bands. That's not the point. The objective is to help everybody. Mostly just to provide bands and audiences with good cohesive shows, to make an event that raises people's eyebrows a bit."[33]

Advertising World Latches onto Indie Rock

Festival promoters are not the only companies trying to profit from indie rock. Advertisers have begun to tap the indie market to find songs to use in commercials and their advertising campaigns. Advertisers use indie rock to make their products seem hip while also giving bands national exposure. For example, the Australian band Jet gained notoriety and fame after their song "Are You Gonna Be My Girl" appeared in the marketing campaigns for Apple's iPod. The song also appeared on the soundtrack for the popular video game *Madden NFL 2004*.

Many artists have been approached to sell their songs for a rather hefty sum of money. In many cases, the money would double or triple the band's yearly income. Sometimes bands accept such lucrative offers in hopes of gaining national exposure, but in other cases, bands have refused to sell their indie credentials.

Indie rock bands the Thermals, Trans Am, and LiLiPUT all refused offers to have one of their songs featured in a Hummer automobile commercial. These and other bands have rejected $50,000 offers from the automaker due to personal principles. Most of the resistance comes from band members' concerns for the environment. Hummers have poor gas mileage, and at a time when dependency on oil has been linked to climate change, many indie musicians do not want their names attached to a product that does not match their personal, political, and environmental views.

Many large companies are turning to indie rock to sell products because they believe the

THE ART OF "SELLING OUT"

Many indie rock bands are accused of "selling out," especially if they start out at an independent record label and later get signed to a major label. Some claim the music of these bands changes due to their label's influence on the band. A band selling their music for a commercial or other form of advertising would also, to many, be seen as selling out. Today, bands are more willing to offer up their music, especially if it is going to help them gain exposure and make money to combat the epidemic in the music industry of dwindling record sales.

In the early 1990s, bands were more hesitant to sell their music for commercial campaigns because they wanted to avoid being called sellouts. They also did not

Matt and Kim gained exposure after offering up their song "Daylight" for a commercial.

popular style of music can help them attract younger, wealthier buyers. Lance Jensen, the former president of an advertising agency representing Hummer, said he and the automaker were not trying to exploit indie music but rather saw it as an opportunity to expose new

INDIE ROCK: FINDING AN INDEPENDENT VOICE

have to rely on this revenue from commercials, since the music industry was thriving. Howard Greynolds, band manager at indie label Thrill Jockey, was there when indie bands Tortoise and Freakwater decided to license songs for Calvin Klein's CK One campaign in 1995. "I remember people calling us saying, 'I can't ... believe they did that, I can't support this band anymore!'" Greynolds said. "We were overly transparent then, we told people, 'Listen, this $5,000 bought them a van.'"[1]

Today, commercialism in music is still looked down upon by some, but not nearly as much as it used to be. As layoffs became prevalent in the music industry and record sales declined, this led to a bigger focus on marketing, advertising, and brands. "All of [a] sudden those were the people at music houses," Greynolds said. "People from your world. They might be feeding you a line ... but there was trust. They were different."[2]

The amount a smaller band can earn from licensing one of their existing songs for a year can add up to between $10,000 and $25,000, and if they compose an original composition, they can earn between $25,000 and $30,000. Indie rockers Matt and Kim, who are also considered indie pop and dance-pop, agreed to let Beta Petrol use their single "Daylight" for a commercial. At first, they were hesitant to sell their music because they knew what negative implications came with it; however, they were also struggling for money. "We thought, maybe no one would ever see the ad, or even recognize the song,"[3] vocalist Matt Johnson said. The opposite happened, and the band gained the exposure they needed to get ahead in the music industry and survive as touring artists: "I have a gold record for that song, and it wouldn't be here if it had never aired."[4]

1. Quoted in Jessica Hopper, "How Selling Out Saved Indie Rock," BuzzFeed, November 10, 2013. www.buzzfeed.com/jessicahopper/how-selling-out-saved-indie-rock?utm_term=.icyvJXJKM#.gtDwMAMWX.

2. Quoted in Hopper, "How Selling Out Saved Indie Rock."

3. Quoted in Hopper, "How Selling Out Saved Indie Rock."

4. Quoted in Hopper, "How Selling Out Saved Indie Rock."

artists: "We just pick music that we like as people. Being a music lover, there's so much interesting work out there, I wonder— why not let people hear it? I don't know, I guess I just want artists to make money. I don't want them to be poor."[34]

INDIE ROCK IS BORN

The Upside of Indie Labels

Despite having the major record industry signing bands that got their start on independent labels, indie labels are thriving. They make up an increasingly larger portion of the music market. With new technology and distribution channels opening up the music industry, independent labels are experiencing a dramatic increase in profits—sometimes as much as 50 to 100 percent each year.

Robby Takac of the Goo Goo Dolls decided to launch his own independent rock label Good Charamel Records in 2003. His original intent was to support bands in his hometown of Buffalo, New York, such as the Juliet Dagger, Last Conservative, and Klear. Takac explained the importance of having indie rock labels amongst major labels:

> *Everything can't be big business. Some things have to come from the heart to find their first steps and this is one of the ways those things get exposed. Major labels like to be involved with proven things, and in this modern world of digital distribution and online social media it's largely up to you and the people who enjoy what you do to prove yourself.*[35]

Another reason indie labels are able to succeed is the fact that their artists' songs will not be heard on commercial radio. Large labels pay radio stations up to $500,000 to have songs from their artists played on national radio. Indie labels are unable to afford to pay promoters that much money to get a song on the air. Thus, they are able to save a lot of money by avoiding commercial radio costs. At a major label, artists are unlikely to make a profit unless they sell at least 1 million albums. In many cases, artists might only earn $1 per album sold, which does not add up to much after expenses such as studio time and limousine rides are subtracted from those costs. In contrast, indie artists might make $5 per album, and if they sell $5,000 albums, they earn $25,000 dollars, which can help supplement their incomes.

This sort of business sense attracts increasingly large numbers to the indie music scene. Many indie labels are able to keep overhead costs down by curbing marketing and using some of the free technology and other platforms available on the internet. Indie labels also work on building relationships with college and public radio stations as well as local retailers, which are often more interested in alternative music.

Another reason indie labels are experiencing growth is that many of them pick up albums that have already been recorded by the artists themselves. In this way, the labels can sometimes avoid recording costs.

Record Label Imitation

Major labels are recognizing the success of indie labels as they begin to control a larger percent of the market share. Many independent labels have been bought by major record companies. Other independent labels are partially owned by one of the majors. Sometimes fans are not even aware that a label that once was independent might have become an affiliate of a major. These buyouts and mergers have created complex relationships between artists, labels, and distribution companies (which are used by both indie companies and major labels).

There are many successful indie labels that have refused to succumb to major-label influence. Saddle Creek, a successful indie label located in Omaha, Nebraska, is one of the leading indie labels that has refused several buyout offers from major labels. Saddle Creek cofounder Robb Nansel talked about the label's decision to remain independent:

> *For me it's always been, "Let's see how far we can take it on our own." I always thought there was no way we could sell 100,000 records. I think I looked up* The Lonesome Crowded West, *that Modest Mouse record, and that's what they sold, so that seemed like the indie peak. But* Lifted [Bright Eyes' 2002 debut album] *sold 250,000. So [we will remain independent] as long as we can continue to move forward and not feel like we're hurting the record.*[36]

In other cases, major labels have begun to adjust their business practices to resemble the structure of independent labels. To do so, they have had to adopt some typically indie characteristics, such as giving the artists more control over the kind of music they produce. This can be both a positive and a negative for bands recording music.

After recording their fourth album, *Yankee Hotel Foxtrot*, Wilco's record label, Reprise, decided not to release it because the label thought it was too experimental and would alienate fans. The executives at Reprise feared that sales would be too low and demanded the band make the album more marketable. Wilco, however, chose not to change the music just to make it commercially viable. Instead, the band bought back the album rights for $50,000 and left the label. Lead singer Jeff Tweedy commented on the band's unwillingness to compromise: "The only negative was that it hurt for a couple of days that someone hated my record so much. We got over it really fast. And then we were just people who play music together. We didn't have a record deal, we weren't touring, we weren't selling anything, and it felt better than ever to be in a rock band."[37]

Wilco did not compromise their experimental way of making music to meet the needs of a record label.

Shortly after leaving Reprise, the band posted the album on their website, streaming the songs for free. The album received positive reviews from fans and critics, and it was not long before another label picked up the album. Ironically, it was Reprise's sister label—Nonesuch Records—which falls under the Warner Music Group, that signed the band. In Wilco's case, it worked in the band's favor to take a chance and make the album without buckling to major-label pressures. In 2011, the band left Nonesuch Records and started their own label dBPM Records, which has released all their records since their eighth album *The Whole Love*. The band's uncompromising ideals and artistic integrity make them something of a legend in the indie rock world despite being signed by an affiliate of a major label.

Some fans and critics worry the more independent labels and major labels resemble each other, the less likely it will be that true independent music will be heard. Ryan Gillespie wrote, "So in a world where the mainstream sounds like the underground and the underground acts like the mainstream, what happens to truly underground music? When major labels buy indie bands by the cart and the indie labels act and operate like major labels, how does a truly independent release get heard?"[38]

The Road Ahead

Despite not having a concrete past or a definitive future, the indie rock genre remains one of the most popular styles of music today. Increasing numbers of indie rock artists are making and recording albums—and not just on independent labels. Today, it seems more acceptable for indie bands, who maintain an image of independence, to sign with a major label if the band has put in years of hard work on an indie label first. The genre itself has become looser in terms of what is considered indie rock. As a result, the future of indie rock looks limitless as indie rock bands and indie labels are adopting and using the technological advances that are affecting the music industry as a whole. Indie rock is ever evolving, and no one is sure how long its popularity will last; however, as of 2018, it seems to be at the forefront of shaping the future of the music industry in the 21st century.

CHAPTER SIX

Indie Rock *Innovations*

Upon entering the 2000s, two areas of the internet experienced exceptional growth: social media and streaming services—two innovations that directly affected the music industry. As social media platforms such as Myspace, Facebook, Twitter, and Instagram became the newest and most popular networking websites, bands began to use them to promote their music and connect with their fans. As music streaming platforms also acquired many subscribers, independent music was able to reach the masses quicker than ever before.

Artists from all musical genres are engaging with new technology, but indie rockers are especially drawn to it because it fits well with the DIY ethic of their predecessors. Sharing music via the internet has spawned a whole new generation of truly independent musicians who can record their own music, burn their own CDs, and distribute their own music, all without the help of any label at all. The debate among music critics and fans is whether the genre of indie rock still refers to music made on independent labels or whether it has become something entirely new.

Arctic Monkeys

In 2006, the fastest-selling debut album in UK chart history came from the English indie rock band Arctic Monkeys. The band's first album, titled *Whatever People Say I Am, That's What I'm Not*, was released in January and sold more than 360,000 copies in less than a week. Within that first week, the band's album sold more copies than the rest of those on the Top 20 album chart combined. What is unique about the band is that they did not make it to the top as a result of a record label's marketing campaign but instead built up their fan base entirely from the internet. The demo CDs the band handed out at shows in 2003 were posted and circulated online—not by band members but by their fans. In 2005,

As of 2018, Arctic Monkeys have released all their albums on the independent record label Domino Records.

with the band's album awaiting release, their debut single "I Bet You Look Good on the Dancefloor" hit number 1 on the UK music charts, followed by their second single "When the Sun Goes Down."

The band eventually signed with independent record label Domino Records. According to a music retailer for the British chain HMV, "In terms of sheer impact … we haven't seen anything quite like this since The Beatles … In the space of just a few weeks the Arctic Monkeys have gone from being relative newcomers to becoming a household name."[39]

Arctic Monkeys are only one of the many independent bands that are achieving success as a result of the internet. The many web-based tools available on the internet are leveling the playing field for indie rock musicians. Social media, digital music websites, online streaming, music blogs, listener recommendations, online music samples, and

INDIE ROCK INNOVATIONS

shared playlists are just some of the tools that are helping bands promote and distribute their music to a much broader audience. The internet has democratized the music industry, replacing traditional modes of distribution and promotion (which were mainly controlled by large record companies) with new technologies that are accessible to people all around the world.

Early Days of Social Media

The internet has become a seemingly limitless resource for indie rock musicians looking for new ways to promote their music. Some of the internet's first social networking websites, such as Friendster, PureVolume, TagWorld, and MySpace, were utilized by indie rock artists as an alternative to traditional promotional methods. These websites allowed indie rock newcomers to share their music with a large audience—without having to be signed to any music label at all. However, many well-established indie acts also recognized the power of these social networking websites to reach audiences. For instance, several popular indie rock groups joined TagWorld in 2005, including Death Cab for Cutie, the Postal Service, and the Shins. At the time, many of these bands were composed of young people who were tapped into the technological world and used the internet as a forum to further connect with audiences.

The Age of MySpace

The first and most popular major social networking website to be utilized by indie rock bands to promote their music was MySpace, which was launched in 2003 by Tom Anderson, Brad Greenspan, Josh Berman, and Chris DeWolfe. By 2006, MySpace was the top social networking website, and in 2007, it was valued at $12 billion.

Although MySpace was originally created for people to meet other people, in 2004, musicians began to design band profiles on the website as well as stream MP3s of their songs. Some bands even allowed their music to be downloaded free of charge. Eventually, bands began to use MySpace to promote albums, announce shows, upload songs and videos, and interact with fans. In early 2005, about 300,000 bands were profiled on the MySpace network; by 2006, that number had doubled to 600,000. In 2006, when MySpace was experiencing its peak in popularity, 29-year-old Anderson described the appeal of the website: "Bands are going to MySpace because it's free and they don't have to know how to do a Web site. But the biggest reason is because there are 43 million people on MySpace."[40]

MySpace decreased the amount of time and money bands spent on development and promotion. In the past, bands spent hours putting up concert posters around town and sending CDs to radio stations. With MySpace, concert and news information about a band was spread through the MySpace community in a matter of seconds. Alex Kerns, drummer and vocalist of Buffalo, New York, indie rock band Lemuria, commented on their past use of MySpace as a promotional tool:

> *Although we were a bit reluctant to start a MySpace at the time, it helped us tremendously. It was still a time where if you didn't tour, you weren't really an active band. For bands like us who were booking our own shows and playing to a handful of people in somebody's basement, it was the perfect resource. It had never been that easy to check out new music. It changed everything.*[41]

Thanks to the exposure they received on MySpace, in 2006, Lemuria was booked for *The Fest* in Gainesville, Florida, where they

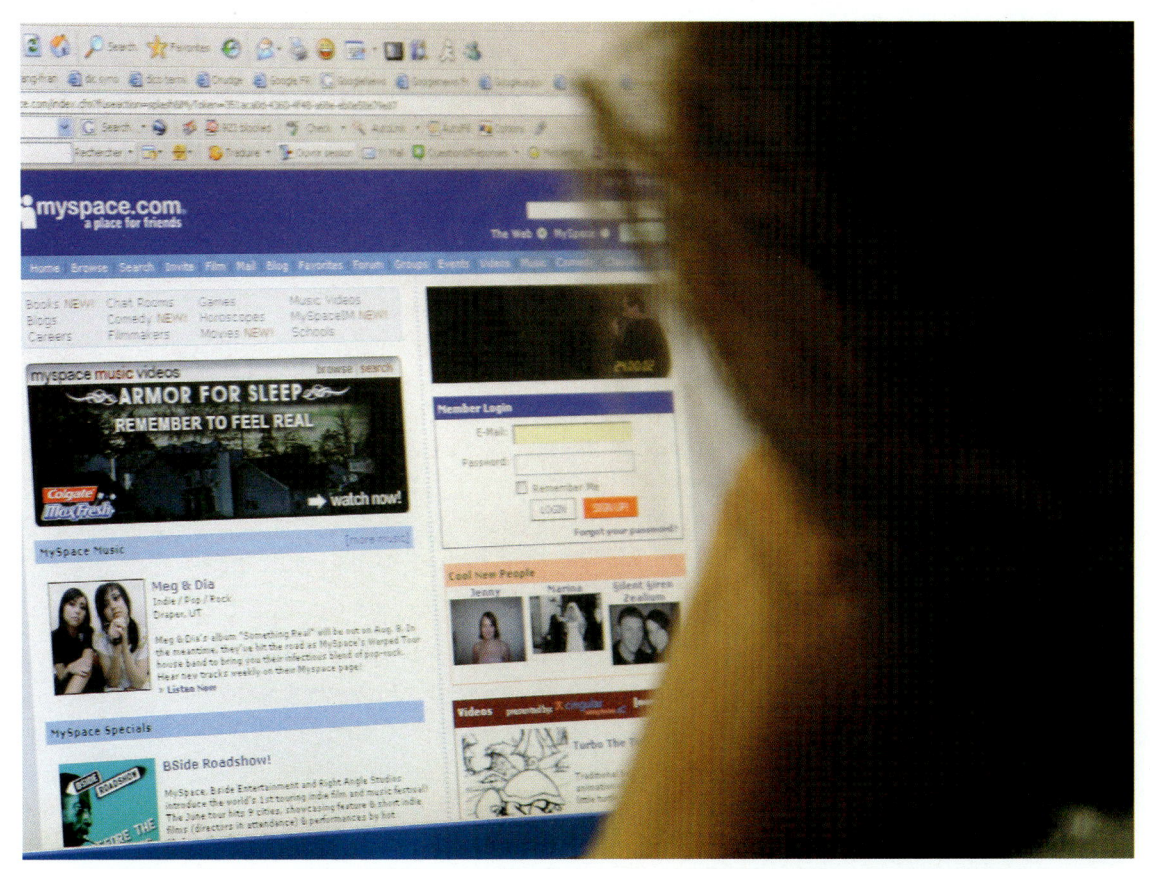

Launched in 2003, MySpace allowed many people to discover new music.

INDIE ROCK INNOVATIONS

played among a lineup of numerous indie bands. "*The Fest* united an international community of bands in a very positive and efficient way,"[42] Kerns said. The band played *The Fest* again in 2018.

Even major recording labels had turned to MySpace to help promote upcoming releases because it was an inexpensive way to reach a large audience. For example, Interscope featured Queens of the Stone Age, Beck, and Nine Inch Nails on MySpace prior to the release of their albums. Interscope even allowed MySpace users to preview songs from the albums. According to DeWolfe during the height of MySpace's popularity, "Labels understand people are spending more time online than on other mediums. Radio is more constrained. MTV is down to about 10 videos a day … MySpace has become the place for awareness of new music and exclusive content. We can point music out ahead of its official release in a very organic way."[43]

After a few years, networking websites such as MySpace and TagWorld became somewhat obsolete, and other websites replaced them. In April of 2008, Facebook surpassed MySpace as the number one social network on the internet. However, MySpace served as one of the first groundbreaking web-based tools, offering bands new ways of thinking about music distribution.

Social Media Innovations

As time went on, social media became more sophisticated, and a variety of options became available beyond just MySpace. Webites such as Facebook, Twitter, Instagram, Tumblr, and more were introduced, and it was almost impossible for bands to not have a presence on many, if not all, of these platforms.

The first time Los Angeles-based artist Jessica Clavin signed with an indie label was with the band Mika Miko, which she played in with her sister Jennifer Clavin from 2003 to 2010. The band was signed to indie label Kill Rock Stars. The sisters broke off from the band and formed Bleached in 2011. When Bleached first signed with a label, they decided to stick with an independent label and chose Dead Oceans. "Indie labels give you that freedom to build and opportunities to express your creative and artistic side," Clavin said. "I feel like I'm constantly growing in my musicianship, having a foundation, but exploring new things."[44]

While in the band Mika Miko, the Clavin sisters depended on other forms of communication outside of social media to spread the word about their band and connect with tour promoters, while Bleached entered a world with more active social media. Jessica Clavin described the advantages of having social media:

Los Angeles indie rockers Bleached have released both of their albums on independent label Dead Oceans as of 2018.

If anything has changed it's been social media. When we first got on Kill Rock Stars I'm pretty sure everything was through email or a phone call. We toured like crazy, and we still do but that's how people saw you. Touring and playing your local venue every weekend with touring bands. The positives are how fast you can communicate and stay in touch with fans. As far as the negatives go, I'm not sure how real things are these days. The live show was so much growing up! Seeing a band and buying the record that day or going to a record store and buying a record you never heard of but the picture looks cool; music was kind of mysterious.[45]

Selling Music Online

In the past, indie rock bands and musicians used touring, word of mouth, fan clubs, and posters to promote their music. Many bands relied on traditional industry channels such as radio and MTV to gain recognition. They would also hand out physical copies of their music, whether it was on CDs or cassette tapes. Today, digital music is the leading format. Thanks to the internet age, there are several online tools that provide new opportunities for independent musicians to share their music with a wider fan base. A greater number of independent artists are heard, while also giving consumers greater choice in their musical selection.

There are several websites that operate virtual storefronts to sell music online. Since 2003, the iTunes Music Store has been a popular website to purchase music. As of 2018, most songs on iTunes cost 99¢, or $1.29 if they are considered more popular, and albums can be purchased typically for a price between $9.99 and $12.99. There is less risk to consumers in buying music by the song because if the purchasers do not like what they hear, they might only be out a dollar, versus the $10 or more they might have lost if they had bought an entire album. With such an easy way to purchase music, people are willing to buy new music that might not be carried in their local record stores or played on commercial radio. For example, iTunes has more than 26 million songs available in its online music library, which is available in 119 countries.

Streaming Services

According to the International Federation of the Phonographic Industry's 2017 Global Music Report, digital music makes up 50 percent of global recorded music revenues. One of the big reasons for this surge in revenue is due to the popularity of music streaming, which experienced a 60.4 percent increase in 2016. Before witnessing the start of this growth in 2015, the global recording industry suffered nearly a 40 percent loss in revenues from 1999 to 2014.

Music streaming services, including Spotify, TIDAL, Apple Music, Amazon Music, and Pandora allow users to listen to music in real time, as opposed to downloading a file onto the computer to listen to later. These services let users listen to what seems like endless amounts of music for a monthly membership fee or free depending on the service. There are more than 100 million users of paid music subscriptions globally with the leader being Spotify as of 2018.

When these music platforms were first introduced, the music industry claimed they were taking away revenue from artists; however, in time, these services actually helped accrue more music sales for artists. Music streaming services also gave artists more control over distribution of their content and improved the listening experience for consumers, giving them more music to choose from at an affordable price.

MUSIC ALGORITHMS

There is an unlimited amount of musical content on the internet, which has found its way into the ears of many music lovers. Depending on a user's musical preferences, they will most likely be more drawn to clicking on their preferred genres when presented with them, which is why music algorithms have become popular on music websites and streaming services.

Alex Kerns of Lemuria explained why even though there is more content on the internet, that does not necessarily mean indie bands will find proper exposure, especially due to the large amount of music available and implementation of music algorithms: "I don't think content is always art. While it is much easier to browse and check out new artists today, it has also become harder to sift through mountains of content on your quest to discovering great art. There are more gems than ever before that are out there to find, but they won't be found if you kick your feet up and let the internet curate your tastes."[1]

Music streaming websites, such as Spotify, TIDAL, and Apple Music, give their users the option to pick a genre of music, which aggregates what they will listen to through music algorithms based on their past listening history. While this may be convenient for the user and introduce them to new music, it limits their exposure to other artists they otherwise might have discovered on their own, but failed to because of their dependence on music algorithms. As the internet has broadened the chance for people to discover new music and listen to a lot of it for free, much of the music they would like is getting lost in the shuffle. There are many effective tools for finding music on the internet, but "a lot of people are no longer operating these modern tools," Kerns said. "Instead they let algorithms automate what they're exposed to, giving them a more homogenized experience of a blossoming world of creativity."[2]

1. Alex Kerns, interview with the author, May 2, 2018.

2. Kerns, interview with the author, May 2, 2018.

In 2017, Hannes Datta and George Knox from Tilburg University in the Netherlands and Bart J. Bronnenberg from Stanford University conducted the study "Changing Their Tune: How Consumers' Adoption of Online Streaming Affects Music Consumption and Discovery." Through their research, they found the increasing use of music streaming websites brought a decrease in use of paid music platforms, such as iTunes. However, the innovation has also benefited indie artists as well:

"In addition to the diminishing consumption share of common favorites, or music superstars, consumers may allocate less of their listening time to their own personal favorite artists," Knox said. Bronnenberg added, "The shift from purchasing music to streaming music levels the playing field to the benefit of smaller producers, indie artists, or smaller labels."[46]

Internet Radio

Internet radio is another online tool that is helping indie rock bands reach new markets and connect with audiences around the world. Bands previously relied on the FM radio market or local college radio stations to play their songs. The internet, however, has changed all of that in recent years. No longer do music fans rely on commercial radio to hear new music. Hundreds of independent radio stations have popped up on the internet to offer alternatives to mainstream music.

Unlike traditional college radio, where broadcasting is confined to small areas (unless the show happens to be syndicated), internet radio is not limited by narrow bandwidths or frequencies. Obscure radio shows playing even more obscure music can be accessed by anyone with a computer. A listener in Australia can log onto internet radio stations streaming music from Canada, the United States, or Great Britain. As a result, internet radio offers indie rock bands greater opportunities to promote and distribute their music to a worldwide audience.

Internet radio shows are becoming increasingly popular, and like college radio, labels are looking to these programs to discover new bands.

Indie Music Blogs, Webzines, and Websites

Music stores, subscription services, and internet radio are just a few of the ways technology has provided indie rock with greater exposure. Like their fanzine predecessors, many websites have created "webzines" to introduce lesser-known or experimental music to listeners around the world. These websites create a community for independent-minded fans in the music industry. Many of these websites provide links to bands' websites, electronic magazines, independent music news, and music samples of featured bands. The goal of many of these websites is to expose people to bands they would not see on television or read about in major publications.

For instance, Obscure Sound is a website that was established in 2006 as a way to provide fans with firsthand information about new indie music. Started by devoted music fan Mike Mineo, Obscure Sound features more than 3,000 independent artists on its website, which includes interviews with artists, album and song reviews, and links to tracks from featured artists. Mineo commented on the importance of indie music blogs and webzines:

> Webzines or music blogs are important to exist, since alternatives (like Spotify "Fresh Finds" and general advertising) are often fueled by one of the major labels, with monetary incentive, while we promote what we enjoy—without monetary incentive playing a role. They benefit independent artists by providing recognition among music fans seeking emerging music.[47]

Another website used to find indie rock music is Hype Machine, which was launched in 2005 by music enthusiast Anthony Volodkin. The website aggregates the most recent songs posted to a selection of music blogs and streaming services and organizes them by genre on Hype Machine's main page. Other websites with similar aggregators and compiled indie rock playlists include Indie Shuffle, Indie Sound, BIRP!, and Indiemono. There are also several music webzines that feature music blogs, such

Indie rock band Clap Your Hands Say Yeah was first discovered on the internet.

INDIE ROCK INNOVATIONS 85

PITCHFORK

At 19 years old, Ryan Schreiber launched a small music webzine, which later became one of the most successful and respected websites for independent music coverage—Pitchfork Media. The website was founded in 1995 in Minneapolis, Minnesota, during Schreiber's time working in a record store. When he was younger, Schreiber noticed there were not many resources on the internet for finding indie music. Instead, a few of his friends had started their own fanzines where they would interview unknown bands and review their music. While Schreiber was drawn to these fanzines, he thought they could use a more opinionated voice:

> The reviews I was reading at the time lacked strong opinions. They were all pretty much reverent. And I thought: "Where's the honesty?" I knew that if I listened to 100 records I was going to dislike at least 20 of them. Also, a lot of the music that was getting popular at that time was second-wave Nirvana, such as Filter and the Deftones. I didn't feel it was independent music. It didn't come from independent labels.[1]

At, first Schreiber was writing two reviews a day, and his website was not getting much attention. By 2010, he had 50 freelance writers and 20 full-time staff workers based in New York City and Chicago, Illinois. Also by 2010, the website had 2.5 million visitors each month and 400,000 visits each day.

Pitchfork is known for their sometimes-harsh reviews, which some claim can destroy an artist's career; however, several artists have had their careers launched by the website as well. Despite the backlash they have received from some artists, the writers at Pitchfork continue to produce a diverse range of music reviews injected with their earnest opinions. "Whereas many blogs are niche-specific or taste-specific, we try to be comprehensive in terms of the independent music world—even if we don't like it," Schreiber said. "We're very, very frank."[2]

1. Quoted in Helienne Lindvall, "Behind the Music: An Interview with Pitchfork Founder Ryan Schreiber," *Guardian*, October 21, 2010. www.theguardian.com/music/musicblog/2010/oct/21/interview-pitchfork-founder-ryan-schreiber.

2. Quoted in Lindvall, "Behind the Music: An Interview with Pitchfork Founder Ryan Schreiber."

as Pitchfork, NME, Consequence of Sound, Stereogum, SPIN, Paste Magazine, Tiny Mix Tapes, Resident Advisor, The Line of Best Fit, and Drowned In Sound. Major music magazines, such as *Rolling Stone*, occasionally cover indie rock artists, but for the most part, they are more focused on mainstream artists.

Many of these independent websites have the ability to launch the careers of relatively unknown bands. For example, in early 2005, the New York indie rock band Clap Your Hands Say Yeah was unsigned and unknown. Without a label, band members had been pressing CDs themselves and selling them at concerts and via the internet. However, the band came to the attention of Dan Beirne, who discovered the group's music while visiting a file-sharing website. He posted a review of the band on the music blog Said the Gramophone. Soon, other blog posts were written about the band; by June, Pitchfork had reviewed a track from the band. A year later, Clap Your Hands Say Yeah had sold 50,000 CDs and had one of their songs played on the NBC sitcom *The Office*.

Music Distribution

Traditionally, independent rockers have struggled to get their music distributed. Many bands might be able to save up enough money to record their music, but it is not always easy to find a label or distributor that will promote the music to record stores. Due to advances in technology on the internet, however, indie labels are finding themselves better equipped to adapt to the changing music industry. By 2016, indie music labels generated $6 billion, or 38 percent of the global music market, according to a report from Worldwide Independent Network. As more bands have utilized the internet as a source for distributing music, it has helped the growth of the indie market.

The increased indie presence is a direct result of companies that serve independent artists who want to distribute their music. Companies such as ReverbNation, TuneCore, MondoTunes, Landr, and Loudr help independent artists on small labels, or sometimes even without labels, negotiate inclusion of indie music within the online music stores. These agencies even negotiate royalty rates.

CD Baby is another website that helps artists without a label find music services to distribute their music. This company is one of the largest and oldest sellers of independent music on the internet and has been helping unsigned bands sell their music online since 1998. It hosts an online retail store where any band can sell their music. The service also helps artists sell their music to streaming services, such as Spotify, Apple Music, Amazon Music, and more. CD Baby only sells music that comes directly from musicians, which allows the musicians to earn a much greater percentage of the music sale.

In its 20th year of operation, CD Baby paid out $80 million to independent artists in 2017 alone, and overall, it has paid out $600 million worldwide to artists since it started. As of 2018, the company distributes music from 650,000 artists, representing artists from 215 territories around the world; this amounts to more than 9 million tracks. As consumers continue to shift toward streaming for their music needs, more indie artists are starting to receive proper compensation for the distribution of their work. "We're excited to see average artists' earnings grow for a third consecutive year due to millions more consumers engaging in music discovery on streaming services," CD Baby CEO Tracy Maddux said. "We're very optimistic about the trend as we continue to lobby for higher per stream rates."[48]

Bandcamp and SoundCloud

Bandcamp and SoundCloud are music platforms, made up of mostly independent artists, offering free music distribution services. These companies do not distribute artists' music to other streaming services, but only allow users to listen to or purchase musical content on their websites.

Since its launch in 2007, Bandcamp has distributed more than $100 million to thousands of artists. The website allows artists to showcase their music through a microsite, in which their music can be uploaded and shared. All the tracks on Bandcamp can be listened to for free, but there is also an option for users to purchase an album or individual tracks at customizable prices. Artists also have the option to sell their music in multiple media formats, such as digitally or on CD, vinyl, or cassette. They also can post upcoming tour dates and links to their official websites and social media websites. Artists can include the option of a subscription service on their page, which allows fans exclusive access to their music and other special features for an annual fee. In 2010, Bandcamp saw a surge in popularity after artist Amanda Palmer left her record label and started selling her albums solely on Bandcamp.

The company also launched Bandcamp for Labels in 2014, which welcomed popular independent labels, such as Sub Pop Records, Epitaph Records, and Fat Wreck Chords, to manage all of their artists from one dashboard, analyze statistics, and utilize other helpful tools. "Bandcamp for labels is a … dream come true!" Bob Lugowe of Relapse Records said. "We can now seamlessly and uber-efficiently manage our entire roster of [more than] 80 bands from one dashboard, plus analyze an unprecedented level of statistics, bulk upload releases, you name it. Truly an essential tool for the music industry in the 21st century."[49]

SoundCloud was launched in

As an indie rock artist, Mac DeMarco was able to find a considerable amount of exposure for his music on SoundCloud.

2007 and allows artists to upload, record, promote, and share their music. Some of the main features of the website include the ability to embed sound files from URLs and post them on social media to improve promotion for artists, who can receive statistics about how many people are listening to their music. On SoundCloud, each track has a ranking; the more users play, repost, and comment on a track, the higher the ranking.

As of 2018, SoundCloud has more than 175 million active listeners. Many users go to SoundCloud to listen to rap and hip-hop artists; however, there are several indie rock artists who have achieved a high status on the music platform as well. Canadian indie rocker Mac DeMarco, who is on the independent record label Captured Tracks, has more than 49,000 followers as of 2018. All three of his studio albums are streaming on SoundCloud, along with two mini albums, and a few demos. Pitchfork has dubbed him the "goofball prince of indie rock."[50]

Indie Rock Artists Today

Current indie rock artists, such as

INDIE ROCK INNOVATIONS 89

Australian indie rocker Courtney Barnett started her own independent record label, Milk! Records.

DeMarco, seem to connect with their fans on a personal and more laid-back level. On his mini-album *Another One*, DeMarco even revealed his home address on the last track. "The way I rationalize it, to have the address you'll have to listen to the album to the very end," DeMarco said. "Second, to even consider coming to my house you have to be a kind of a superfan. And thirdly, it's in such a weird part of New York that if they actually get there, they deserve a cup of coffee."[51]

Another popular indie rock artist on the scene today is Car Seat Headrest, which was started by songwriter Will Toledo, who after years of self-releasing his own albums on Bandcamp, is now part of Matador Records. He came up with the name "Car Seat Headrest" after he decided to record the vocals of his first few albums in the back seat of his car for privacy. He is known for his DIY ethic and has received accolades by Pitchfork, *Rolling Stone*, and several other music publications.

Courtney Barnett found huge success with her debut studio album, *Sometimes I Sit and Think, and Sometimes I Just Sit*, which landed atop several Billboard charts. She released the album on her own independent label Milk! Records in March 2015 and first played songs from the album at *South by Southwest* music festival that year. Barnett's DIY ethic inspired her to create her own label, which she started with money she borrowed from her grandmother. Her first release on the label was her EP *I've Got a Friend Called Emily Ferris* in 2012. In 2015, Barnett won the Australian Music Prize, and she was nominated for Best New Artist at the 2016 Grammy Awards.

Indie Rock's Legacy

As other music genres did before it, indie rock seems to be paving the way to leave a legacy; however, there is no telling how much longer the genre will be around. For many artists within the indie rock genre, the music undoubtedly comes first, and then sometimes comes fame. Several artists never find a widespread audience, while others happen to catch the eye of influential music industry leaders who propel them directly into the mainstream.

How to properly define the term "indie rock" is still up for debate. Does "indie rock" still only refer to music recorded on independent labels? Is it a type of sound or style of music? What about the bands that self-produce and self-record? What about bands that start out independent, but end up becoming famous in the mainstream? While there is no real set definition for the music genre, indie rock keeps appearing on music charts and gaining more and more fans every day.

Advances in technology have made releasing music for indie rock artists much easier and have created almost limitless possibilities. The internet has introduced social media, music streaming services, and music distribution services, such as Bandcamp and SoundCloud, which have allowed artists to promote and release their own music all without being tied to a record label. Gone are the days of being dependent on being signed by a major label; independent artists now have other options of getting their music heard by the masses.

Indie rock is the latest phase of youth-oriented rock music. First came punk, then college rock, then grunge, and now indie rock reigns supreme. Perhaps in a few years a new catchy phrase will be coined to describe whatever new trend in music comes along, or maybe indie rock will continue to separate off into subgenres. Regardless of what happens in the future of indie rock, one thing is for sure: Indie rock has the power to bring exposure to independent artists, giving them a chance to have their music heard.

Notes

Introduction:
Indie Rock Phenomenon
1. Ryan Hibbett, "What Is Indie Rock?," *Popular Music and Society*, 2005.

Chapter One:
Punk Rock Attitude
2. Greil Marcus, *In the Fascist Bathroom: Punk in Pop Music, 1977–1992*. Cambridge, MA: Harvard University Press, 1993, p. 2.
3. Hibbett, "What Is Indie Rock?"
4. Quoted in Legs McNeil and Gillian McCain, *Please Kill Me: The Uncensored Oral History of Punk*. New York, NY: Grove Press, 1996, p. 18.
5. Quoted in McNeil and McCain, *Please Kill Me: The Uncensored Oral History of Punk*, p. 118.
6. Quoted in A. S. Van Dorston, "What Are the Politics of Boredom?," *Fast 'n' Bulbous* music webzine, February 20, 1990. fastnbulbous.com/punk/#One.
7. Quoted in James Gregory, "Interview: Buzzcocks," Pitchfork, February 20, 2006. pitchfork.com/features/interview/6263-buzzcocks/.
8. Quoted in Steven Wells, *Punk: Young, Loud & Snotty*. New York, NY: Thunder's Mouth, 2004, p. 7.
9. Quoted in Gregory, "Interview: Buzzcocks."

Chapter Two:
The Power of DIY
10. Quoted in Bob Stanley, "The Birth of the Uncool," *Guardian*, March 30, 2006. www.theguardian.com/music/2006/mar/31/popandrock1.

11. Quoted in Graham Lock, "Desperate Bicycles," *New Musical Express*, October 14, 1978.
12. Quoted in "How to Make a Fanzine!," Punkjourney.com, accessed on May 16, 2018. www.punkjourney.com/fanzines.php.
13. Michael Azzerad, *Our Band Could Be Your Life*. New York, NY: Back Bay, 2001, p. 10.
14. Quoted in Dave Thompson, *Alternative Rock*. San Francisco, CA: Miller Freeman, 2000, p. 52.

Chapter Three: Explosion of College Rock

15. Hugo Lindgren, "I Love the Eighties," *New York*, accessed on May 16, 2018. nymag.com/nymetro/arts/music/pop/reviews/12305/.
16. Quoted in Meredith Levine, "At WYBC, Old Guard and Ratings Push Clash," *Yale Herald*, March 1, 2002. www.yaleherald.com/article.php?Article=292.
17. Quoted in Levine, "At WYBC, Old Guard and Ratings Push Clash."
18. Quoted in Steve Pond, "In the Real World," *Rolling Stone*, December 3, 1987. www.rollingstone.com/music/news/r-e-m-in-the-real-world-rolling-stones-1987-cover-story-20110921.
19. Quoted in Heidi Sherman, "Sebadoh Slip from Indie Shackles," *Rolling Stone*, February 22, 1999. www.rollingstone.com/news/story/5923105/sebadoh_slip_from_ indieshackles.

Chapter Four: The Emergence of Grunge Music

20. Quoted in Kurt St. Thomas and Troy Smith, *Nirvana: The Chosen Rejects*. New York, NY: St. Martin's, 2004, p. 6.
21. Quoted in St. Thomas and Smith, *Nirvana*, p. 16.
22. *Hype!*, directed by Doug Pray, 1996 (Los Angeles, CA: Republic Pictures).
23. Quoted in Thomas L. Bell, "Why Seattle? An Examination of an Alternative Rock Culture Hearth," *Journal of Cultural Geography*, Fall/Winter 1998.
24. Quoted in Michael Azzerad, "Grunge City: On the Seattle Scene," *Rolling Stone*, April 16, 1992. www.rollingstone.com/music/news/grunge-city-the-seattle-scene-19920416.
25. *Hype!*, directed by Doug Pray.

26. Quoted in Steve Gdula, "Archers of Loaf Keep DIY Attitude," *Rolling Stone*, September 18, 1998.
27. *Dig!*, directed and produced by Ondi Timoner, 2004 (Los Angeles, CA: Interloper Films).
28. *Dig!*, directed and produced by Ondi Timoner.
29. *Dig!*, directed and produced by Ondi Timoner.

Chapter Five:
Indie Rock Is Born

30. Quoted in Andrew Brown, "Despite Digital Downloads Making Headway into CD Sales, Customers Young and Old Are Still Attracted to Vinyl," Collecting Vinyl Records, December 15, 2008. collectingvinylrecords.blogspot.com/2008/12/despite-digital-downloads-making.html.
31. Jim DeRogatis, "Emo (The Genre That Dare Not Speak Its Name)," *Guitar World*, 1999. www.jimdero.com/OtherWritings/Other%20emo.htm.
32. Quoted in "Vans Warped Tour: All Things Must Come to an End," VansWarpedTour.com, November 15, 2017. vanswarpedtour.com/2017/finaltour/.
33. Quoted in Jordan Kurland, "Snap, Crackle, and Noise Pop," *SFGate*, February 26, 1997. www.sfgate.com/style/article/Snap-crackle-and-Noise-Pop-3133552.php.
34. Quoted in Otis Hart, "Bah Hummer: Indie Rockers Reject Big Money from the King of Gas Guzzlers," Austin360.com, February 21, 2006. www.austin360.com/music/content/music/stories/2006/02/22hummer.html.
35. Robby Takac, email interview with author, April 23, 2018.
36. Quoted in "King of Indie Rock," *Rolling Stone*, January 13, 2001. www.rollingstone.com/news/story/6822956/king_of_indie_rock/print.
37. Quoted in Joan Anderman, "Wilco's Jeff Tweedy Has a Restless, at Times Alienating Creativity That Makes the Shy Songwriter an Indie-Rock Icon," Boston.com, August 6, 2004. archive.boston.com/ae/music/articles/2004/08/06/wilco146s_jeff_tweedy_has_a_restless_at_times_alienating_creativity_that_makes_the_shy_songwriter_an_indie_rock_icon?pg=full.
38. Ryan Gillespie, "Bring on the Major Leagues," PopMatters, January 25, 2006. www.popmatters.com/060126-indiemusic-2496104363.html.

Chapter Six:
Indie Rock Innovations

39. Quoted in "Arctic Monkeys Make Chart History," BBC News, January 29, 2006. news.bbc.co.uk/1/hi/entertainment/4660394.stm.
40. Quoted in Josh Belzman, "Bands and Fans Singing a New Tune on MySpace," MSNBC.com, February 13, 2006. www.msnbc.msn.com/id/11114166.
41. Adam Kerns, email interview with author, May 2, 2018.
42. Kerns, email interview with author, May 2, 2018.
43. Quoted in Belzman, "Bands and Fans Singing a New Tune on MySpace."
44. Jessica Clavin, email interview with author, May 4, 2018.
45. Clavin, email interview with author, May 4, 2018.
46. Quoted in Institute for Operations Research and the Management Sciences, "Music Streaming Sites Benefit Indie Singer at the Expense of Top 100 Artists," Phys.org, December 15, 2017. phys.org/news/2017-12-music-streaming-sites-benefit-indie.html.
47. Mike Mineo, email interview with author, May 1, 2018.
48. Quoted in Dan Rys, "CD Baby, Now In Its 20th Year, Says It Paid Out $80M to Indie Artists in 2017," *Billboard*, March 6, 2018. www.billboard.com/articles/business/8232210/cd-baby-20th-year-paid-80-million-indie-artists-2017.
49. Quoted in RiffYou, "Fat Wreck, Epitaph, Sub-Pop Get Bandcamp Pages," Riffyou.com, December 17, 2014. www.riffyou.com/fat-wreck-epitaph-sub-pop-get-bandcamp-pages/.
50. Quoted in Evan Minsker, "Mannish Boy," Pitchfork, March 26, 2014. pitchfork.com/features/cover-story/reader/mac-demarco/.
51. Quoted in Ben Kaye, "Mac DeMarco's New Album Ends With His Home Address and an Invite for Coffee," Consequence of Sound, July 23, 2015. consequenceofsound.net/2015/07/mac-demarcos-new-album-ends-with-his-home-address-and-an-invite-for-coffee/.

Essential Albums

Publisher's note: Some albums may contain strong language or explicit content.

Arcade Fire
Funeral (2004)

Arctic Monkeys
Whatever People Say I Am, That's What I'm Not (2006)

Bikini Kill
Revolution Girl Style Now! (1991)

Bright Eyes
I'm Wide Awake, It's Morning (2005)

Car Seat Headrest
Teens of Denial (2016)

Courtney Barnett
Sometimes I Sit and Think, and Sometimes I Just Sit (2015)

Daniel Johnston
Hi, How Are You (1983)

Death Cab for Cutie
Plans (2005)
Transatlanticism (2003)

Dinosaur Jr.
You're Living All Over Me (1987)

Fall Out Boy
Take This To Your Grave (2003)

Hüsker Dü
Zen Arcade (1984)

Mac DeMarco
Salad Days (2014)

Modest Mouse
The Lonesome Crowded West (1997)

Neutral Milk Hotel
In the Aeroplane Over the Sea (1998)

The New Pornographers
Mass Romantic (2000)

Nirvana
Bleach (1989)

Pavement
Slanted and Enchanted (1992)

Pixies
Surfer Rosa (1988)

R.E.M.
Murmur (1983)

The Replacements
Let It Be (1984)

Sleater-Kinney
Dig Me Out (1997)

Sonic Youth
Daydream Nation (1988)

The White Stripes
White Blood Cells (2001)

Wilco
Yankee Hotel Foxtrot (2002)

For More Information

Books

Earles, Andrew. *Gimme Indie Rock: 500 Essential American Underground Rock Albums 1981–1996*. Minneapolis, MN: Voyageur Press, 2014.
   This book dissects 500 essential albums from 308 of indie rock's most well-known bands from the 1980s and early 1990s.

Goodman, Lizzy. *Meet Me in the Bathroom: Rebirth and Rock and Roll in New York City 2001–2011*. New York, NY: Dey Street Books, 2018.
   This book provides an intriguing history of the New York City rock scene after the September 11, 2001, terrorist attacks.

Gordon, Kim. *Girl in a Band: A Memoir*. London, UK: Faber and Faber, 2016.
   Kim Gordon's memoir takes a deeper look into her time playing in the band Sonic Youth in the 1980s and 1990s and balancing the many other facets of her life during this time.

Turgeon, Richard. *Indie Rock 101: Running, Recording and Promoting Your Band*. Burlington, MA: Focal Press, 2013.
   This book is a DIY guide for anyone interested in starting a band. It gives insight on recording music, promoting, selling music, making videos, and more.

Websites

Bandcamp
bandcamp.com/
> Bandcamp allows users to listen to free music from artists of all genres, who can post their music without needing the permission of a record label. There are also links to artists' official websites and feature articles.

Pitchfork
pitchfork.com/
> Pitchfork provides that latest music news and music reviews from various independent and popular music artists.

ReverbNation
www.reverbnation.com/
> This online music platform provides tools and technology for independent artists to use to manage their careers.

SoundCloud
soundcloud.com/
> Independent artists can use this online audio distribution platform to post their music and have it exposed globally, while fans can discover music from various artists.

Under the Radar
www.undertheradarmag.com/
> This online music magazine regularly posts music reviews, features, and news about indie music artists.

Index

A
Albini, Steve, 65
Alice in Chains, 55
Alternative Tentacles, 34
"Anarchy in the U.K." (Sex Pistols), 12, 22
Arcade Fire, 67–68
Archers of Loaf, 57, 62
Arctic Monkeys, 76–77
Azerrad, Michael, 34

B
Bandcamp, 88, 90–91
Barlow, Lou, 48–49
Barnett, Courtney, 90
Barsuk Records, 6
Beck, 59, 80
B-52s, The, 18
"Big Three" record companies, 8–9
Bikini Kill, 56
Black Flag, 35, 37, 42
Bleached, 80–81
Blondie, 18, 33
Brand New, 66
Bratmobile, 56
Brian Jonestown Massacre, 60
Bright Eyes, 63–64, 73
Built to Spill, 55, 59
Buzzcocks, 21, 28–29, 52

C
Car Seat Headrest, 90
cassette tapes, 48, 81
CBGB, 16, 18–19, 24, 33
C86 compilation, 48
Clap Your Heads Say Yeah, 85, 87
Clash, The, 21–22, 26
Cobain, Kurt, 43, 51, 53, 55, 61
Cocteau Twins, 41
College Media Journal (CMJ) Music Marathon, 67
Cramps, The, 18
Cure, The, 38, 44

D
Damage, 34
Dandy Warhols, 58–59
Dashboard Confessional, 66
Deal, Kim, 42–43
Death Cab for Cutie, 6–7, 63, 78
Decemberists, The, 8, 59
DeMarco, Mac, 89
Desperate Bicycles, 28–29
Diggle, Steve, 21–22
Dinosaur Jr., 38, 43–44
Dischord, 34–36
disc jockeys (DJs), 44
do-it-yourself (DIY), 26–27, 29–31, 34, 37, 48, 57, 64, 76, 90
Dunn, Ged, 33

E
emo, 65–67

F
Facebook, 76, 80

Fall Out Boy, 66
fanzines, 26, 30–34, 36, 48–49, 53, 84, 86
Frontier, 34
Fueled By Ramen, 67

G
Ginn, Greg, 35, 37
grunge, 11, 50–51, 53–57, 59, 62–64, 91
Guided By Voices, 62

H
Hell, Richard, 18–19
Hole, 61
Holmstrom, John, 33
Hüsker Dü, 36, 39, 46–47

I
Instagram, 76, 80

J
Jamming, 30
Jensen, Lance, 70
Jet, 69
Jimmy Eat World, 66–67
Joan Jett & the Blackhearts, 18
Johansen, David, 16
Johnston, Daniel, 54–55
Jones, Steve, 22

K
K Records, 59
Kristal, Hilly, 18

L
Lemuria, 79, 83
LiLiPUT, 69
London's Outrage, 30
Love, Courtney, 61

M
MacKaye, Ian, 35
Matt and Kim, 70–71
Maximumrocknroll, 34
Max's Kansas City, 16, 33
McLaren, Malcolm, 19
McNeil, Legs, 33
Meat Is Murder (The Smiths), 45
Merge Records, 59
Mika Miko, 80
Minor Threat, 35, 42
Misfits, The, 18
Modest Mouse, 59, 73
Moore, Thurston, 18
MTV, 46, 54, 56, 63, 80–81
Mudhoney, 53, 55
music streaming services, 76, 82–83, 91
MySpace, 76, 78–80

N
Neutral Milk Hotel, 41
New Order, 45
New York Dolls, 16, 18–20
New York Rocker, 34
Nirvana, 43, 50–51, 53–55, 61, 86
Noise Pop, 69
North by Northwest, 67

O
Oar Folkjokeopus, 30
120 Minutes, 46

P
Paramore, 66
Pearl Jam, 55
Peel, John, 44
Perry, Mark, 30–31
Pitchfork, 85–87, 89–90
Pixies, The, 38–39, 41–43
Plans (Death Cab for Cutie), 6, 63

Pretty Vacant: A History of Punk (Strongman), 24
psychedelic music, 11
punk, 11–14, 16–24, 26–28, 30–34, 36–39, 41, 43–44, 47–48, 52, 57, 64–66, 91
Punk (magazine), 33–34

R
Ramones, The, 16–19, 21, 30, 46
Reed, Lou, 14, 33
R.E.M., 44, 47–48
Replacements, The, 36–37, 39, 44, 47
Riot Grrrl movement, 56–57
Rock Scene, 34
Rotten, Johnny, 12, 22
Rough Trade, 29, 32–33, 45

S
Saddle Creek, 73
safety-pin ethic, 18–19
Screaming Trees, 55
Search & Destroy, 34
Sebadoh, 43, 48, 62
selling out, 48, 59–60, 70–71
Sex Pistols, 12, 21–24, 26, 28, 33, 52
Sideburns, 30–31
Simple Machines, 57
Siouxsie and the Banshees, 38
Slash, 34
Sleater-Kinney, 56–57, 59
Smith, Patti, 16, 18, 24, 33
Smiths, The, 32, 38, 44–45
Sniffin' Glue, 30–31
Sonic Youth, 18, 38–39
SoundCloud, 88–89, 91
Soundgarden, 53, 55–56
South by Southwest, 67–68, 90
Spiral Scratch (Buzzcocks), 28
Spotify, 82–83, 85, 87
Spungen, Nancy, 24
SST, 34–36, 39
Strongman, Phil, 24
Strummer, Joe, 22
Sub Pop, 34, 53, 88

T
Taang!, 34
Takac, Robby, 72
Taking Back Sunday, 66
Talking Heads, 16, 18
Television, 16, 18–19
Thermals, 69
TIDAL, 82–83
Touch & Go, 34
Trans Am, 69
Transatlanticism (Death Cab for Cutie), 6
Twitter, 76, 80

U
Ugly Things, 30
Used, The, 66

V
Vans Warped Tour, 66
Velvet Underground, 14–15
Vicious, Sid, 24

W
Warhol, Andy, 14
Wax Trax, 34
White Stripes, The, 8
Wilco, 63, 73–74

Y
Yankee Hotel Foxtrot (Wilco), 74
Yellowcard, 67

Picture
Credits

Cover (guitar) JRP Studio/Shutterstock.com; cover (background), back cover, pp. 3, 4, 6, 12, 26, 38, 50, 63, 76, 92, 96, 98, 100, 103, 104 Ksenija Toyechkina/Shutterstock.com; pp. 7, 8 Wendy Redfern/Redferns/Getty Images; pp. 15, 17 Michael Ochs Archives/Getty Images; p. 19 William LaForce Jr./NY Daily News Archive via Getty Images; p. 20 Bettmann/Bettmann/Getty Images; p. 23 Virginia Turbett/Redferns/Getty Images; p. 28 Fin Costello/Redferns/Getty Images; p. 31 Estate Of Keith Morris/Redferns/Getty Images; p. 32 Ian Dickson/Redferns/Getty Images; p. 35 Erica Echenberg/Redferns/Getty Images; p. 37 Paul Natkin/Getty Images; p. 39 Anthony Pidgeon/Redferns/Getty Images; p. 41 David Tonge/Getty Images; p. 42 JA Barratt/Photoshot/Getty Images; p. 45 Pete Cronin/Redferns/Getty Images; p. 47 Paul Natkin/WireImage/Getty Images; p. 51 Jeff Kravitz/FilmMagic, Inc/Getty Images; p. 54 Ebet Roberts/Redferns/Getty Images; p. 56 Bob Berg/Getty Images; p. 58 David A. Smith/Getty Images; pp. 61, 74 Mick Hutson/Redferns/Getty Images; p. 64 Robin Little/Redferns/Getty Images; p. 66 Theo Wargo/Getty Images for iHeartMedia; p. 68 Tony Woolliscroft/WireImage/Getty Images; p. 70 Timothy Hiatt/Getty Images for Pandora; p. 77 Andy Willsher/Redferns/Getty Images; p. 79 NICHOLAS KAMM/AFP/Getty Images; p. 81 Monica Schipper/Getty Images for Panorama; p. 85 Phil Bourne/Redferns via Getty Images; p. 89 Michael Tullberg/Getty Images; p. 90 Rene Oonk/Shutterstock.com.

About the Author

Vanessa Oswald is an experienced freelance writer and editor who has written pieces for publications based in New York City and the Western New York area, which include *Resource* magazine, *The Public*, *Auxiliary* magazine, and *Niagara Gazette*. In her spare time she enjoys dancing, traveling, reading, snowboarding, and attending live concerts.